Tell Your Heart to Beat Again

Tell Your Heart to Beat Again

Resuscitating, Repositioning and Renewing Your Spiritual Life

Joanne Ellison

Unless otherwise indicated, Scripture quotations are taken from the Holy Bible, New International Version®, NIV®. Copyright © 1973, 1978, 1984, 2011 by Biblica, Inc.™ Used by permission of Zondervan. All rights reserved worldwide. www.zondervan.com
Scriptures are also taken from: THE ENGLISH STANDARD VERSION. © 2001 by Crossway Bibles, a division of Good News Publishers. The Holy Bible, King James Version (public domain). The Message by Eugene H. Peterson. © 1993, 1994, 1995, 1996, 2000. Used by permission of NavPress Publishing Group. All rights reserved. The NEW AMERICAN STANDARD BIBLE®, © The Lockman Foundation 1960, 1962, 1963, 1968, 1971, 1972, 1973, 1975, 1977, 1995. Used by permission. The NEW KING JAMES VERSION. © 1982 by Thomas Nelson, Inc. Used by permission. All rights reserved. Holy Bible, New Living Translation. © 1996, 2004, 2007. Used by permission of Tyndale House Publishers, Inc., Carol Stream, Illinois 60188. All rights reserved.

Library of Congress Cataloging-in-Publication Data
ISBN: 0997124326
ISBN 13: 9780997124323
Printed in the United States of America

Acknowledgements

This book is dedicated to my father, Dr. Peter Gazes and my husband Dr. Blount Ellison, both cardiologists. Their passion for healing the physical heart has shaped my passion for healing the spiritual heart.

Contents

Introduction

BELOVED FRIENDS, IT is time to tell our hearts to beat again. The body of Christ is weary and battle worn. The church has been lulled to sleep from pure exhaustion and discouragement and needs to be resuscitated.

I have been in ministry for thirty years, and I see an awakening in the body of Christ. I see a picture of the church yawning as if awakening from a long winter's nap. And while we napped, the world changed. I believe that the church is returning to its first love, awakening to the profound truth that *while we were yet sinners—messy, complicated, untrusting, and unloving—God sent His Son to die for us.* His radical love is awakening us. The truth of His Word is causing us to rise up, embracing His love and carrying it out to a lost, broken, and dark world.

Both my father and husband are cardiologists. As I thought about the state of the church today, I began to see a lot of parallels between the health of the church and the health of the human heart. If we ignore our physical health whether through poor diet, inactivity, or excessive stress, our physical health suffers. So too if we ignore the vital practice of drawing near to God and abiding in Him, our spiritual lives suffer. We are missing the life of Christ, the compelling love of God that the world so desperately needs.

It is time for the church to wake up, rise up, and grow up in His Word. We have flat lined, and our hearts have lost hope and become discouraged. We've been lulled to sleep, but it's now time to hear a new song in our hearts. We are not called to be settlers. We are called to be pioneers, joining the saints who went before us, carrying the torch of hope to the world.

One of the issues we face as we awaken is our need to de-clutter our lives. We must make space for God to be our first love, our first priority. We are too busy, stressed, always pressed for time. What has overtaken *your* life?

I liken what has happened to the church to a loaded potato. Over the years the baked potato has undergone quite a transition, from a simple baked tuber to what is now known as the "fully loaded potato." To be "fully loaded" requires adding ingredients to the potato--sour cream, chives, cheese, bacon, and anything else you can think of that would enhance the flavor. The problem is that sometimes if we add too much, rather than enhancing the flavor of the potato, we camouflage the flavor. The original taste and texture of the potato becomes lost in the barrage of ingredients competing for the attention of our taste buds. As I pondered writing this book, I realized that our Christian lives could become like the overloaded potato. The original flavor or authenticity of the life of Christ in us becomes lost in the muddle of activity and pressure of life. What if you were to order a loaded potato and say, "Loaded potato, please—but hold the potato?" We would be left with the accessories but not the core ingredient. We can make the same mistake in the Christian life: "Give me Jesus *plus*—perfect relationships, more money, more time, more joy, less fear and anxiety." What happened to simply "Give me Jesus"? He is the main ingredient, the One who is the Source of life, hope, peace, and joy. But we ask for the potato, only *hold* the potato.

Now, don't get angry with me. We are only at the introduction of the book. Give me time to unfold what I mean. As Christians, we have become much like the world, embracing the idea that we must strive more, work harder, be better, and our Christian lives will take wings. Chasing the things of the world distracts us. But Jesus said this: *"Seek My kingdom and My righteousness, and all these things will be added"* (Matt. 6:33, paraphrased). What things? The things that add flavor to life. Jesus said to keep Him as our focus, seeking Him, delighting in Him, and He will take care of the rest. He did not mean that life would not be stressful or busy or full of the cares of the world. He simply meant that He has our backs. He can take care of all things, and He promises to take the burdens and give us His peace. Life in Christ is not meant to be one more thing we add to our busy lives. It is meant to be simple, keeping Him at the center, as we work and live from a place of resting in Him.

Friends, we live in a world filled with stress and fear, with so much that we have no control over, and frankly but for God would be downright terrifying. Yet, we are called to be the hope and light of the world. It is time for the church to wake up, rise up, and grow up, centered on Christ alone. This book is about being overwhelmed by the love of God rather than being overwhelmed by the world. It is about making space for the One who can keep us focused, at peace, and filled with joy so that our hearts can beat again. My hope is that as you take this journey with me, you will find a new way of living, that you will be fully loaded with the extravagant love and grace of Christ, not overloaded with activity, pressure, and fear. If we are to be the hope of the world, then we need to be different from the world, and it is only by His grace that we can shine and hold out a new way of living that is winsome and desirable.

In a video interview, singer Randy Phillips, of contemporary Christian music's Phillips, Craig and Dean, shares the story behind the trio's song "Tell Your Heart to Beat Again." A surgeon had just performed heart surgery on a patient. After a successful operation, he knelt down beside his patient, took off his surgical mask, and whispered, "Tell your heart to beat again." And it did. This story inspired Randy Phillips to write the song as a commission to the broken hearted. Even though God, the Great Physician and Surgeon, has saved and repaired us, sometimes we have to tell our own spiritual hearts to beat again.

Joanne Ellison

Tell Your Heart to Beat Again

Forgiven
If only you'd forgive yourself
You've been made new
But you're standing where you fell
Because when you look in the mirror
It seems like all you ever see
Are the scars of every failure
And the you that you used to be

Tell your heart to beat again
Close your eyes and breathe it in
Let the shadows fall away
You'll live to love another day
Yesterday's a closing door
And you don't live there anymore
So say goodbye to where you've been
And tell your heart to beat again

Forgiven
Just let that word wash over you
It's alright now
Love's healing hands have pulled you through
So, get back up and take step one
And now your new life has begun
And know that if the Son has set you free
Then you are free indeed!

Tell your heart to beat again
Close your eyes and breathe it in
Let the shadows fall away
You'll live to love another day
Yesterday's a closing door
And you don't live there anymore
So say goodbye to where you've been
And tell your heart to beat again

Hope is reaching from a rugged cross
Where a perfect love recaptured all the innocence that's lost
And mercy's calling from an empty grave
So lift your eyes to heaven
And hear your Savior say

Tell your heart to beat again
Close your eyes and breathe it in
Let the shadows fall away
You'll live to love another day
Yesterday's a closing door
And you don't live there anymore
So say goodbye to where you've been
And tell your heart to beat again[1]

PART I

Wake Up—Resuscitate

CHAPTER 1

The Weary Church

WE NEED TO face the music. The church is weary. We have been *desperately trying to fight* our *own* battles *when the Word makes clear* that it is God alone who fights our battles. (See 1 Sam. 17:47; 2 Chron. 20:15). We are weary from the battle. I don't know about you, but there are times when I think that I am the savior of the world. Honestly, that attitude is not just mine. I see churches filled with people who are worn out from trying to bring the gospel to a hostile world. We are exhausted in our jobs and relationships. Our hearts, once pumping strong, have flat lined.

I remember when as a child my father would take me with him to the office on Saturdays to catch up on his work. When I got bored, he would stop and teach me how to read electrocardiograms, or EKGs. "What does it mean when the zigzag line goes straight?" I'd ask. "Does that mean the patient died? Did his heart stop?" Dad never tired of answering my questions.

The path of our spiritual lives often looks like the reading of an EKG. The enemy's tactic is to wear down the saints and flat line our spiritual lives, but God continues to draw us to Him with cords of love. His radical love can awaken us from a deep sleep or resuscitate us from death to life.

Now it's time to take off my mask and tell you my flat line story. When my husband and I had three children under the age of six, we had the opportunity to live in Germany. I fantasized about how awesome it would be--even romantic--to live in a foreign country. I read travel brochures and dreamed of what life abroad would be like. My expectations were unrealistic. Nevertheless, off we went.

The first three months, we lived in the small village of Lambsbourne where no one spoke English. I was lonely, missed my family in the states, and resented my husband who gleefully went off to work every day. What happened to the beautiful pictures of what life would be like in a foreign country? After three months in a very lonely and dark place, I met an amazing German woman named Marika. Marika and her husband Otto spoke English, and Marika reached out to me. Actually, she rescued me. She knew of a house for rent closer to the army base in a community where English was commonly spoken. We moved there, and then I thought my fantasy picture-book life abroad would begin.

Sadly, though my neighbors were awesome, I was still lonely and sometimes depressed at home alone with three small children. In came my friend Marika, to the rescue again. She invited me to her Bible study (in German) which was my lifeline at the time. I could follow along in my Bible. Nevertheless, I hit a wall.

One day, I opened the windows in search of relief from the blazing heat. Unfortunately, there were no screens on the windows, and we lived next to a horse farm. The sweltering heat sapped my energy; the children were cranky and fighting; the diapers piled up; and the horse flies from the farm next door invaded my kitchen like a scene from Alfred Hitchcock's movie "The Birds." I began to lose it. After killing thirty-two flies (oh yes, I counted every one of them), I sat in the middle of my kitchen floor and broke down crying. The children sat there and stared at me, as I stared at the bloody bath of flies on the floor counting them one by one.

At just that moment my husband came sauntering in with a friend he had invited for dinner. And calling out my name.... you guessed it he found me on the floor looking insane with flies all around me and the children staring in disbelief. Thirty years later, I remember vividly the look on my husband's face—a complex mixture of fear, horror, anxiety. And his friend…. Well, we won't go there. Let's just say, he left suddenly.

Friends, we all have times when we lose it or we have flat lined, and our hearts need to be resuscitated. Only Jesus can do this for us. We have to run to him. Spouses, friends, or co-workers can help only so much. Spiritual resuscitation comes from Jesus, the only One who can breathe life back into us.

Now, here is the simple truth in all of this: God has a plan for you. He has your back. And He is still on the throne. He fights your battles and refreshes your weary soul. He is for you and not against you. He is your best Advocate, and He knows you better than anyone else. His love brings life to the weary. He is altogether different from the people we encounter. In His presence there is fullness of joy. (See Ps. 16:11). So what's the problem? The problem is we need to make space for Him in our overloaded lives. Otherwise the burdens of life and the cares of the world, will undo us, destroy us, or cause us to go underground.

The good news is that God has not given up on us or His church. We are the hope of the world—God carriers, in the sense that the Holy Spirit lives within believers. Our part is simply to receive God's love and spill it out on a broken world. But the enemy has blinded us, and discouragement looks for a place to settle in our hearts. We have listened to the enemy's lies and let him in. Our guard is down because we are weary.

Come to Me

Jesus understood our dilemma. He knew that life would throw a lot of hard balls and sticky balls. His words to us echo throughout the ages: *"Come to me, all you who are weary and burdened, and I will give you rest"* (Matt. 11:28). Is your soul drained? Then come to Jesus and spend time with

Him in His Word, in prayer. I call this the secret place, the place where my overloaded life is set aside and Jesus draws near. It is the place where our hearts begin to beat again.

My childhood fascination with the heart has grown into an interest in the parallels between the physical and the spiritual heart. We each need a spiritual electrocardiogram to see the condition of our hearts. For some of you reading this, your spiritual hearts are weakened and battle weary.

The Message translation perfectly describes our condition: *"Are you tired? Worn out? Burned out on religion? Come to me. Get away with me and you'll recover your life. I'll show you how to take a real rest. Walk with me and work with me—watch how I do it. Learn the unforced rhythms of grace. I won't lay anything heavy or ill-fitting on you. Keep company with me and you'll learn to live freely and lightly."* (Matt. 11:28–30)

Friends, we must wake up from our weary state. We need to come to the Lord and allow Him to remove our heavy burdens, our ill-fitting garments. This is done simply by spending time with Jesus and releasing to Him the burdens we have been wearing. He ignites our hearts with passion for Him, removes our burdens, and gives us His peace. Who doesn't want to live "freely and lightly?" We all do. We all yearn for simplicity. We yearn for a life filled with "unforced rhythms of grace."

I sometimes find myself going back to memories of days when life seemed simpler and uncomplicated. Often those memories are of times with my grandparents, when we did the simplest of things together that had significant impact.

I remember gardening with my grandfather--the joy of checking on each plant to see the progress, clear the weeds, smell the herbs. His garden looked out over the marshlands and was to me the most peaceful place on the earth. Working side by side with my grandfather was what I picture heaven will be like. God, working on His beautiful creation with me beside Him in awe listening, watching, taking it all in. Somehow on this little patch of earth, I worked out with my grandfather all of my little girl stress, heartbreak, and frustration. He would listen mostly but that was the point. He would *listen*. He made me feel as though I was the only person on earth and he only had ears for me. I was a bit of an insecure little girl, overweight and not very attractive. I was surrounded by beautiful smart sisters and friends, and I recall feeling as though I could never measure up. But my grandfather, Papoo, (grandfather in Greek) loved me just as I was. I felt free to be myself and not have to prove myself. Papoo in turn would share things with me that were close to my heart. He intuitively knew my thoughts and my heart-felt issues and offered wisdom and support. (I also think he relished the opportunity to practice his English!) My memories of those days take me back to a simpler time when problems were never insurmountable because my grandfather would solve them all.

My grandparents were born in Greece, and I recall the stories of how my grandfather came to the United States to create a better life. He asked his family to send him a bride from Greece once he was established in the States. How different things are today. People meet and get married on *The Bachelor* and *The Bachelorette*!

But my favorite memory takes me back to the simplicity of Grandfather's garden, a place where I knew the unstressed, unforced rhythms of grace. It seems counterintuitive to talk about simplifying through gardening. Wouldn't it be easier to go to the grocery store and pick up a package of fruit or vegetables? Probably so, but true simplicity is found in the preparation and nurture of the garden and in the time spent with a truly wise man. How true this is for our overloaded lives.

In our weariness we have chosen the path of least resistance, but often the path of nurture is the most beneficial. The time spent in tending the garden created a song and a rhythm of grace in my heart as I enjoyed the benefits of gardening and the undivided attention of my grandfather. And that song still plays in my heart today, a song of yearning for simplicity. So it is in our spiritual land. An unforced rhythm of life can be found as we spend time with God, unrushed, allowing the Holy Spirit to till our hearts, lifting our burdens from us, giving us His peace, and breathing life into our weary souls.

What has made you weary in life? What has caused your heart to flat line and your life to become dull and routine? The Lord is beckoning you to come home—to His home, the place of abiding.

Abide in Me, and I in you. As the branch cannot bear fruit of itself, unless it abides in the vine, neither can you, unless you abide in Me.
-John 15:4 NKJV

CHAPTER 2

Lulled to Sleep

I WANT TO suggest to you that the church has been lulled to sleep. Let's take a look at some of the changes just in the last decade. Technology alone has enhanced globalization. With only a click we are able to access data across the world. We can communicate in ways we never dreamed. Across the world we see tension from terrorist groups that have disrupted world peace and security. We are so inundated with information from around the world, that we have become desensitized to the needs around us. Meanwhile, in America, the land of opportunity, we have great prosperity; and our sense of entitlement grows, even as we experience an underlying sense of emptiness. This sense of emptiness has led us on a search to fill the void with things other than the Lord. We have become disconnected from our families as we drift from the Lord. Families and family values are losing significance as the world seems to be spinning out of control. We are on overload between world events and internal family crises. Our jobs weary us, our homes are not safe havens, and world news causes us stress. So in a sense, the church, the body of faithful believers in Christ, exhausted and feeling defeated, has been lulled to sleep. In our discouragement we have gone underground.

But I believe this season of sleep is coming to an end. The church is waking up and rising up to be the city set on a hill. (See Matt. 5:14). Once again, under pressure, the church revives, recognizing that God has the answers and that only through knowing Him and connecting with

Him can we find peace. We are beginning to hear a new song—a song of revival. The Lord is calling us to come away with Him to the secret place, His garden, where He bids us to abide in Him. There He sets before us a banqueting table filled with the encouragement in His Word. Much like the way I enjoyed spending time with my grandfather relishing in the fruits of our labor and the beauty of creation, the Lord wants to call us away to the garden of His Presence where we can enjoy one another and the unforced rhythms of grace.

"Like an apple tree among the trees of the forest, so is my beloved among the young men. In his shade I took great delight and sat down, and his fruit was sweet to my taste. He has brought me to his banquet hall, and his banner over me is love." (Song of Solomon 2:3–4 NASB)

God wants us to spend time with us and shower us with good things. So if the table is filled with His promises, why do we find ourselves starving? He beckons us to come in and feast with Him. In this day of awakening, the church is discovering that Jesus is our only peace and source of contentment.

Years ago, when I was newly married, everything was so fresh and exciting. Young love is exhilarating. But after forty years of marriage, I have discovered that it is the depth of the relationship that brings me peace, security, and contentment. Young love fades, but true love, deep love, endures. Jesus is calling His church back to its first love in Him. Our initial exhilarating encounters with God lay a foundation for the deep love which develops over the years from knowing His faithfulness in the good times, bad times, and everything in between. We learn of His steadfast love as the Promise Keeper, and the love and forgiveness grows in us a deep desire to press on. His faithfulness replaces our discouragement with courage.

Take for example Peter, the wildly impetuous disciple who encountered Jesus as a fisherman. He ran after Him, finally denying Him, and, ultimately filled with the Holy Spirit, became bold for Him. When people witnessed Peter's healing of the blind man at the gate Beautiful they knew He had been with Jesus. Jesus, empowers, gives us courage, and makes us bold.

The church is awakening and finding itself in a dark world. I believe the church is recognizing its calling to wake up and offer the light of the world. Light will always dispel darkness, but darkness cannot dispel light. We, as the church, are called to bring the light to a dark world, to bear the image of Jesus who is the hope of the world.

The church has been persecuted since its very first century, but the church's finest hours have always been under persecution. The first-century church grew not *in spite of* persecution but *because of* persecution. Over the centuries it grew during the darkest times.

When I think of the church, I am reminded of a magnificent gemstone. In jewelry stores, gems are often placed on black velvet because against the darkness of the cloth, the stone shines brightly. Church, it's time to wake up and shine.

———

The age of reason, the scientific revolution, and humanism have caused mankind to become self-sufficient. But God, who created humanity, looks for a people who are God-reliant. In our self-sufficiency we have succeeded spectacularly to advance our world, but internally our souls are empty. Only God can fill the void. And He stands knocking at the door of our depleted hearts. We can choose to ignore Him. We can crack the door a bit and peek through at Him. Or we can invite Him in to a place of fellowship. *"Look!"* he beckons. *"I stand at the door and knock. If you hear my voice and open the door, I will come in, and we will share a meal together as friends"* (Rev. 3:20 NLT).

Western secularism has removed God from the public life. This culture insists that Christ be removed from your private life as well. But without God we must face down the pressures and stress of life alone. Without God we stare at death, and we are hopeless, like sheep without a shepherd. Our souls despair. But when we invite Christ in, He comes in to dine and fellowship with us. Sharing a meal is an intimate act. Jesus bids us open the door to intimacy with Him.

———

He makes me lie down in green pastures. He leads me beside still waters.

-Psalm 23:2

Every year when I go for my annual medical examination, I expect the nurse to tell me that my heart rate is very slow, because it always is. In fact, one year the nurse remarked that I was barely alive. In the medical world, a slow heart rate is a good thing, but if our hearts stop, via a cardiac arrest, we might die.

Spiritually speaking, our spiritual pulses, when we are trusting the promises of God's Word and the safety of His faithfulness, have an even, steady heart rate. Our assurance is in the Lord, and we know the truth of Jesus' words.

Jesus said, *"My yoke is easy and my burden is light"* (Matt. 11:30). I find comfort in knowing that we will find rest for our souls when we surrender our burdens to Him. Easier said than done, right?

As a young mother and wife, surrounded by dirty dishes and dirty diapers, I was stressed and exhausted. I lived to get a good night's rest, knowing that the next day would be more of the same. I loved being a mother, but it is frontline duty. There is no rest for the weary, and the only hope for survival was to have eight hours of sleep. Instead I was always sleep deprived and irritable. Can anyone relate? I wasn't always the train wreck that I was in my flat line story; however, I was often so worn out that I wondered if I could just get on a train and never come back. Sometimes I think we women think we have to appear to have it all together. The truth is we never do and never will. As mothers, we often feel guilty wondering if we ruined our children's self-esteem or knowing we lost it yet another time... or wondering where the day went and feeling guilty over not having quality time with them? I will never forget how inadequate I felt when I went with another young mom for our field day excursion. When it came time to have our picnic and open our children's lunchboxes, I noticed my friend's was packed neatly with all of the food groups. Appealing and delightful right? My daughter to my dismay, at that moment, was opening hers, and I re-member thinking I have to do something quickly--distract the other mother, offer to buy my daughter lunch at the cute little snack bar nearby. And then the unthinkable happened. She opened her lunchbox and out spilled cheerios (ok it wasn't breakfast, but it was all I had) and some slices of cheese, and who knows what else. All I remember is the feeling of shame and inadequacy as the other mother looked at the contents spilling out of the lunchbox. I had visions of this same mother fixing a hot breakfast, and all I recall is tossing cheerios into the back seat for my daughter to catch in her mouth. (It was a little game we played). So there it is. We do try and compare ourselves to those who appear to have it all together. But you know what? Years later as I observe my beautiful grown- up kids, I know they were not harmed by my imperfect lunches or mothering techniques. They didn't always eat organic, and there were days when I gave in to Twinkie bars, and cookies.... You get the picture.

Again, I recall living in Germany and being exhausted. (And yes my cute husband was still skipping out the door to work every day leaving me behind with these three monsters. Ok, I was tired, and it seemed at the time that they were little monsters).

We lived near a church. I went to bed that first night, with hopes of sleeping uninterrupted, but, at four o'clock in the morning, the bells chimed from the church tower. Then *every* morning at four, the bells chimed, and I would wake up unable to fall back asleep.

After several nights of this, I questioned the Lord about why I now had to deal with this. I was a young Christian, a God seeker, and a desperate stay-at-home-with-three-small-kids mom. There is something about being desperate that ignites Christ-seekers. And the answer surprised me. I sensed the Lord was asking me to pray at that hour. You can be sure that that was not the answer I was looking for. More sleep deprivation? But after a few nights passed, I broke down and began to use that time to meet with God. To this day, I recall it being the sweetest time of intimacy with the Lord. It was quiet and peaceful. It became my secret place with God. The best part is that from the first occasion of spending this early hour with the Lord, I woke up refreshed and renewed in mind, soul, and body. During those early-morning times, scriptures would come to mind, and a new thirst for God's Word grew. I began to journal what I felt the Lord was saying to me.

As I grew in my faith, I discovered that true rest comes from spending time in the presence of God. My spiritual pulse was steady and strong. My irritability improved, for which my husband was grateful, and my days became filled with purpose. Again, it seems counterintuitive to get less sleep and suddenly feel rested. I began to wake up spiritually despite getting less sleep at night. The world demands that we get on its treadmill and wear ourselves out with doing, with performance, and with self-reliance, but God leads us beside still waters, not racing waters, and bids us to come sit with Him.

Here is the problem we all face. The Lord is calling us to Him, but we would rather sleep. We are worn-out from our days with dirty diapers and laundry, demanding jobs, and other responsibilities. I can so empathize with the feeling of being overwhelmed and exhausted. Some days it felt like I would never make it to the end, and I would collapse in a heap at the end of the day feeling like I had nothing left to give. Waking earlier to pray seemed ludicrous. But God did the unthinkable. He took my simple choice to give into the bells and draw near to Him in that time, and He began to transform me on the inside. He took that simple act of obedience and blessed it. Even though I had less sleep, the fruit of the Holy Spirit was evident in my life to my husband and children. And I was a better wife and mother because of it.

We are lulled to sleep from sheer exhaustion. But God bids us come to the still waters and have our souls restored. I sometimes wonder if the enemy has sent out an assignment that says, "Go after the most vulnerable, sleep-deprived, exhausted, weary women, and offer them a soft bed in which to lie."

The temptation is great. But when we get in bed with the devil, he only serves up trouble. There is no peace for our souls as he spews out his lies: "If only you were a better employee, or a better wife, or a better mother." He is wearing down the saints (that's us, as believers) because if we are worn-out, he has his best chance at lulling us to sleep. He cringes at the thought that we might stay awake, pray, commune with God, and be refreshed.

The foundation for my Christian walk was built during my years in Germany when the church bells chimed four times and I was awakened from a deep sleep. The Lord was saying to me, *"But all things become visible when they are exposed by the light, for everything that becomes visible is light. For this reason it says, 'Awake, sleeper, and arise from the dead, and Christ will shine on you.' Therefore be careful how you walk, not as unwise . . . but as wise"* (Eph. 5:13–14 NASB).

Could He be saying the same to you?

CHAPTER 3

Letting Go of the Old

ONCE WE ARE aware of our need for soul restoration, we must also recognize that some things just have to go. We are playing an old, tired song, and the new song needs to be released. We've got to let go of the old and embrace the new. Back to the analogy of the physical heart, we sometimes allow things to build up in our lives that cause a blockage. Just like a blockage that can cause a heart attack, a buildup of activity or negative thought patterns can lead to spiritual sickness or death. In the medical world, patients who have several blocked arteries around their heart can be treated with coronary artery bypass surgery or have springy lattice tubes called stents inserted to open clogged arteries.[2] A successful procedure results in the restoration of the heart to normal healthy functioning. Friend, it may be time for your spiritual heart to have a stent inserted so that your spirit can be revitalized. The definition of revitalize is "to impart new life or vigor to; restore to an active or fresh condition."[3] What has caused you to lose your vigor in life? Perhaps it is simply your need to let go of the old and embrace the new. The Lord can unblock the most stubborn and resistant artery. Are you willing to surrender your spiritual heart to the Great Physician?

The first of this year, after reading my daily scripture, I sensed the Lord speaking to me: *"Let go of the old and embrace the new."* I joked with my husband about it and told him that if he didn't straighten up . . . as he is one of the oldest things I have around, I might need to get rid of him! As the year has progressed, I have been intentional about discerning which things I have on life support, things that have sucked the life out of me.

Seasons change, and sometimes a change in season requires releasing things that may have been good and even life-giving. While releasing good things is sometimes difficult, if we refuse to let them go they begin to steal our joy. We can also miss out on the next thing God intended for the new season because we tenaciously held onto a good thing when he had something better for us. If we have spent time nurturing that relationship with the Lord, we know Him and can trust in His goodness so that obedience becomes a more natural response. Furthermore, when we have that depth of relationship with Him. we are not so busy that we miss His leading in this area.

One of the changes that I made in the New Year was to be more intentional about taking care of myself by eating better and exercising more. I had to let go of some of my habits and embrace the new. There were changes in relationships that required shifting and a significant letting go of things in ministry. Each loss led to a better gain. I had to examine those things that I had kept on life support because I thought I did not have a choice. For example, I had been involved in some projects, and my part was completed; however, I held on to my involvement out of a false sense of commitment. I did my part. Why did I hang on? Guilt, people pleasing, sense of feeling needed? When I spent time with the Lord examining what was on my plate, I knew that that was one of the things I needed to release. Friends, we need to be aware of which responsibilities we may be keeping on life support. When something no longer brings me life or when I dread a commitment, I know I need to seek the Lord about letting go. I have found that although many things are challenging that the Lord calls me to do, when He has called me to cooperate with Him, His Holy Spirit breathes life on projects that otherwise would be burdensome. Jesus was clear that His yoke is easy and His burden light (Matthew 11:30).

Here is the problem and the challenge that we all face. If we keep things on life support that God never intended, we begin to operate on our own. We roll up our sleeves and make it happen all the while becoming resentful. Now here is an interesting thought. When we become resentful doing something we were never called to do or doing things past the season we were called to be involved, our spiritual hearts can become hardened, maybe even bitter.

I equate this state of the spiritual heart to the condition of the physical heart called arteriosclerosis or hardening of the arteries. The definition of arteriosclerosis is the thickening of the walls of arteries. This process gradually restricts the blood flow to one's organs and tissues and can lead to severe health risk.[4] Our spiritual hearts similarly can have hardening of the spiritual arteries impacting our walk with the Lord. We can lose sight of our need to spend time with the Lord. We begin operating on auto pilot rather than being led by the Holy Spirit and filled with His power. And what happens next? We burn out physically, spiritually and emotionally. Not good. Especially when Jesus longs for us to draw near to Him to be refueled.

Is there anything you sense that is wearing you out, any area in which you are simply going through the motions repeating something that is lifeless? If you are already so overwhelmed with life, it may seem counterintuitive to add time and make space for God. But His easy yoke will lead you to freedom. Sometimes it is as easy as simply recognizing that you are weary and asking why. The body of Christ is being revitalized for such a time as this. The world needs a vigorous active, fresh church.

In John 16:7 Jesus said that He must leave the earth, but He would subsequently send His Spirit to guide us into all truth. As Christians, our ability to discern the different seasons in our lives is dependent on the guidance of the Holy Spirit. We may think we have something on life support, only to find out that God is still in it; but we have been disobedient, and now the task feels heavy and burdensome. Or we may think it is time to let go of something, but the Lord actually means to surrender it to *Him*, not necessarily that the season is over. But there is also a third scenario. It may be that you are in a season where the Lord is telling you that it is time to let go and move on. Discerning which season you are in is dependent on the surrendering to the Holy Spirit. So I begin each day saying, "Here I am, Lord, the one that You love. I surrender my day to You. Holy Spirit; you are now in the driver's seat." I take this practical step as a way of reminding myself that I am not in charge.

Last year I decided to try something. I wanted to see if surrendering as I did every morning made any difference in the outcome of my day. So I held out my calendar before the Lord each morning, actually my iPhone, and said, "Lord, have Your way in my day. Holy Spirit, You lead. Cancel appointments if need be; shift my day, that I might see You at work." That is a simple enough prayer.

What transpired was amazing. After three months, I went back and looked at my schedule. I left all entries on my calendar even when things were canceled and shifted to see what the Lord was doing. Over and over again, I saw a pattern of my plans being disrupted by God's plans. I noticed that canceled meetings had afforded me the opportunity to spend time with someone in need. A meeting would be canceled and, remarkably, someone would call. With my tight schedule I knew it could only be God having His way. The simple test has shown me that when He is in charge, my days flow easily in the hands of Christ. Stress is reduced, and my spiritual pulse is steady. Try it. It works!

Now let's talk about how to gracefully let go of something you have kept on life support. First, you need to ask yourself why you are still doing the same thing, expecting different results. Are you weary and feeling burned-out? Then consider the first two scenarios I mentioned. Are you worn from doing something because you are actually in disobedience? Or are you worn-out because you need to surrender and let God handle the situation, not necessarily that you can or should walk away? If you have discerned that it is neither of these, then consider the third option. You are weary because the life expectancy of what you are doing in a job, a relationship, or whatever has expired. You are keeping it on life support, but it's time to let go. Let me give you an example.

When my children began to leave for college, I was in a fit. I did not want to transition out of motherhood as if you ever could. But at the time, letting go felt like death to me. To be honest, I didn't have too difficult a time when my first child left the nest because I still had two more at home. Even though I missed her so much that it ached, it seemed as though the season would be fine. Each child thereafter who left made me want to hold on tighter. I cried for months when my second one left, and I wanted to cling to my third as if my life were ending. Can you relate? This season was one of the most heartbreaking, terrifying, don't-want-to-let-go times in my entire life. Women, we were created to be nurturers. My life was grounded in my need to nurture, and raising my children had fulfilled this need. And now what? I was not just losing my job raising my children; I was losing my identity. Who was I now? I was totally lost. And no one knew that my heart was bleeding because I could not share my pain without feeling that the life was being sucked out of me. Perhaps some of you reading this are thinking, "That won't be me; I am so ready to be an empty nester." Wait and see. It's painful to join that club. But here is the good news. My life did not end. In some ways it began anew. It was my time to enter into another season of motherhood, that of letting my children grow up but never letting them go entirely. We never do. The Lord graciously led me into a sweet season of using what I learned raising my children to become a ministry leader. The tools that motherhood had provided were invaluable.

Even though letting go was painful, the time was right for my children to leave. Their leaving and my letting go were healthy and even necessary. Now I am in a new season, with grandchildren, and I realize that the very gifts I had to surrender have come back to me in spades! They all came back, with more of them.

The truth is, what we truly surrender, what we let go of in its proper season, we gain in the big picture. Letting go of my children enabled them to find their own lives and purpose. When they returned, things were different, but in many ways so much better. They went away still as kids, and came home as adults ready to face the world. The next season of letting them go to their respective spouses and new homes and lives was difficult, but again, letting go of that season enabled me to have a fresh, new season with them, one in which they began to appreciate me in ways I never imagined.

Entering into new seasons is much like the performance of a flying trapeze artist in the circus. The acrobat must let go of one rope to grab hold of the next one. For a brief moment it must be frightening—but only for a moment, until she gracefully grasps the next one. We all go through seasons of having to let go. God will throw you a new rope. Of course, you may refuse to catch it, wishing to hold on to the old and fearing the new. Having developed a relationship with Him based on love and trust in His character can enable us to gracefully release the last season and embrace the new, much like the acrobat trusting her partner to release the first rope so that she can gracefully move from the first rope to the next without falling.

Letting go not only involves the seasons of our lives. Sometimes we simply need to let go of old thought patterns, thoughts we have lived with and kept on life support but that have been detrimental to us and our relationships. This way of thinking has caused our hearts to lose hope. I refer to these as stinkin' thinkin'.

Beloved fellow Christians, we must begin to recognize that a battle for our minds is raging. The warfare is all around us; the battlefields are where we are, in the now, here, every day. The world tells us lies, and the enemy gets us to agree; he throws stresses, inconveniences, and hardships into our paths as roadblocks. He hides in the dark-thought strongholds we have allowed in our lives, and then at the right opportunity, he jumps out to divert us, mislead us, cause us to stumble. He loves our stinkin' thinkin' because when we are engaged in it, we are in agreement with him. The enemy is the father of lies (see John 8:44). Some lies have been embedded in the womb of our thoughts since birth. Others are hidden until the enemy draws them out at the time he chooses.

Rats, Lies, and Liberation

Recently my clothes dryer smelled really bad. I mean, it stunk. When the repair technician took a look, he found a rat's nest so huge that it had wrapped itself completely around the inside of the dryer and burned the motor. Sometimes negative thoughts invade our minds and dominate our thought life causing us to burn out. Stinkin' thinkin' destroys. The enemy's lies consume us and lead us to make bad decisions. Think back to a time when you believed a lie. Consider how your buying into that lie affected your behavior. Isn't it remarkable how even the smallest "nest" in our thoughts can cause us to react in ways we later regret? When we agree with the enemy's lies, we are headed for destruction. Agreement with God's truth sets us free.

> *"Remember not the former things, nor consider the things of old," God tells His children. "Behold, I am doing a new thing; now it springs forth, do you not perceive it? I will make a way in the wilderness and rivers in the desert"* (Isa. 43:18–19 ESV).

It's time to forget the "former things" including the lies and the "stinkin' thinkin'" we have embraced. Instead, let us wake up and be revitalized with a vibrant beat in our spiritual hearts.

CHAPTER 4

Recognizing and Releasing Stress

WE ARE ALL familiar with tension. Life simply can be stressful. Research has been done to determine the correlation between stress and heart disease, which is the leading killer of Americans. What we do know is that stress may affect factors that increase the risk for heart disease such as high blood pressure, cholesterol levels, physical inactivity, and poor eating habits (contribution made by my brilliant cardiologist husband). We all are under a certain amount of stress such as deadlines, responsibilities, and health issues. It is a fact of life that not one of us is immune to stress. To live stress free we would have to be in heaven, and since you are reading this book, you are not there yet. We live here on earth where there is no stress-free zone. So the question is, how is one to handle stress as a Christian? Let's begin with defining *stress*.

Stress is a state of mental or emotional strain or tension resulting from adverse or very demanding circumstances. We have already said that life can be demanding and can take its toll on us. Now, for a moment, let's enter into the days when Jesus walked the earth, sent by the Father. Were His days stressful? Were they demanding, and did people drive Him crazy? Was His mission on earth so intense that He went to bed every night hoping that the next day would be better? As the One who tells us that *our* burdens can be light when we give them to Him, how did *He* bear up under the pressure of being the Son of God, sent to save the world? Here are some snapshots from His life on earth. I have taken the liberty to write the story as if we were traveling with Him on the dusty roads of the Middle East, witnesses of His Mission on earth.

At twelve years old, Jesus recognized that His mission was to set the captives free. Let's join him in Nazareth, the place where He had been raised, in the synagogue on the day He recognized His mission.

———

It is the Sabbath, and suddenly someone hands Jesus a scroll. *Why are they handing the scroll, the reading for the day, to a young boy?* We wonder. *Could it be that He is someone special? Why didn't they give it to one of the rabbis?*

Jesus takes it as if it is no big deal, as if it is an everyday occurrence to be in the holy temple and be asked to read God's Word. He opens it and reads from Isaiah 61: "'The Spirit of the Sovereign Lord is upon me, for the Lord has anointed me to bring good news to the poor. He has sent me to comfort the brokenhearted and to proclaim that captives will be released and prisoners will be freed'" (vv. 1–2 nlt). He closes the scroll, and all eyes are on Him. Who is this man-child?

And then the unforgettable happens. We hear Him speak: "Today this Scripture has been fulfilled in your hearing" (Luke 4:21 nasb).

What are we to make of this? Full understanding is not ours. But we listen. We wait. His words ring in our ears as a young boy acknowledges that He is on mission from His Father. Perhaps He is too young to recognize that this sobering moment, acknowledging He has work to do on earth, will end at the young age of thirty-three at the hands of a cruel death.

Time has passed, and Jesus is now entering into ministry. He is thirty, and the tension is mounting. We follow Him to a wedding in Galilee—where He turns water into wine. There is mumbling in the room, and then a series of questions as His life as Savior unfolds before men. Who is this? He heals the paralytic, opens deaf ears, and cures the lepers. He preaches in a boat. He walks on water. All in a day's work fulfilling His mission.

Was Jesus stressed? I do not think so. Of course He must have been tired from His long days, yet He made space in His life to be with His Father. (See Luke 5:16). He sought His Dad in prayer knowing that He could only do what the Father told Him to do. He went to His Dad to be refreshed and to see what His Father was doing. He worked from a place of resting in the security that His Dad knew best, that His Dad would help Him in His mission as the Savior.

There were *times* of stress, however. In the Garden of Gethsemane, when death was crouching at the door, He pleaded with His Father to take the cup of death that He faced from Him. But He trusted His Father to do what was best and willingly offered His body as a sacrifice for our sins. (See Matt. 26:39). He handled the stress simply by trusting the Father.

When I was in my early years of ministry, I attempted something that without God I would have failed. In my morning Scripture reading, as I read Psalm 133, I sensed the Lord speaking to me:

"A Song of Ascents, of David. Behold, how good and how pleasant it is for brothers to dwell together in unity! It is like the precious oil upon the head, coming down upon the beard, even Aaron's beard, coming down upon the edge of his robes. It is like the dew of Hermon coming down upon the mountains of Zion; for there the LORD commanded the blessing—life forever." (Ps. 133:1–3 NASB)

The Lord was speaking to me about unity. Several years before this I had started a community-wide Bible study called Drawing Near to God, and it had been difficult to get various churches to come together under one roof. Little by little, the Lord had His way, and people from different denominations and no denomination came to the study. As I read through the first few verses of this psalm, the words "for there the LORD commanded the blessing" rang through my head. Unity in Christ through the power of His Holy Spirit brought blessing. This word brought new purpose to what I had begun.

Of course, my recognition of this word and the newfound determination to keep pressing on with the study would not bless old "red legs" (that's the devil). I received a phone call from someone who said, "Who do you think you are? Trying to do this?" At the time I remember thinking, *I don't think I am anyone except someone who is trying to be obedient to a call.* I had a difficult time shaking those words, and with that came the next assault. "Should you be teaching as a woman?" And then came the lies: "She is a religious fanatic." One by one the words caused intense stress. I had a choice. Press on or cave. By the grace of God and with the support of caring Christian friends, I pressed on.

Persecution my dear sisters is stressful. And if you are a card carrying lover of people or desire to please others, it can be a killer. I remember feeling like Elijah in his little cave. He had had seen the demonstration of God's power against the god Baal and his followers. Elijah was bold for God and expected His God to show up, and He did. But Elijah ran when he heard that Miss Jezebel (King Aram's wife) was ticked off. She was determined to have him hunted down and killed because he had killed all the prophets of Baal, and they were her strong men (or so she thought). So Elijah finds himself in a cave, and God asks him what in the world he is doing in there. Elijah wines a bit about God forsaking him (how quickly he had forgotten God's faithfulness), and God breaths life on him in just a whisper. Read the story. I think you can relate. We all can because we forget how God is for us and not against us and that persecution comes, and we run and hide. But God pursues us and finds us in the cave.... and sometimes has to drag us out of our self pity into the light of His Presence.

Beloved people, the enemy does not play fair. His mission is to kill, steal, and destroy. (See John 10:10). But God sent His only Son on a mission to set captives free. And my job is to participate with the mission of Christ. The stress of it all could have stopped the purposes of God for that Bible study, and your stress threatens to do the same.

To stand against the enemy's destructive mission, we must recognize symptoms of stress. Some of the physical symptoms, according to MedicineNet, include sleep disturbance or changes in sleeping habits, muscle tension, muscle aches, headache, gastrointestinal problems, and fatigue.[5] Stress takes a toll on our bodies! Stress also takes a toll on us spiritually. We may feel as though God has abandoned us, or we may become so fatigued that we are unmotivated to pursue our relationship with Christ. We may lose a desire to read the Word, pray, or be in fellowship with other Christians. We may isolate ourselves, resulting in the enemy's attacking us in our vulnerable state, whispering his lies. But there is a better way to withstand the assaults, and that is to make space for God to deal with our stress. Call on fellow Christ-followers to pray for you and with you. Seek counsel and soak in God's promises for you in His Word. You may be so stressed you cannot do much, but you can read a promise a day until you spiritual tank begins to fill back up again.

A few years ago, I was on my way back from speaking at a conference, and my tire began to go flat. I was in a remote area and was afraid to stop so I continued on the wobbly tire very slowly until I could get to a gas station to get some help. When I arrived, the attendant told me that I should have stopped because by continuing on the flat tire, I had damaged my rim, which would cost me more to fix than a flat tire. How like that we all are where stress is concerned. We run on "tires" that are slowly leaking, and rather than stopping and getting some help, we do more damage to ourselves. It is far better to deal with stress when the symptoms appear than to allow stress to have its way and cause more damage.

Worshiping Jesus is the answer to our stress. Worship takes the focus off of our circumstances and places it on God. Worship is a stress buster, and yet it requires that we lay aside our busyness and make space for God.

In *How to Worship Jesus Christ*, pastor Joseph Carroll tells of a friend of his who was traveling in Japan. When he stopped to have his oil checked, a great army descended on the man's car, offering all kinds of service—washing his windshield, even cleaning his tires. But when he left, he realized that the one thing he needed—oil—he did not get.[6] Do you ever feel that way, that you do everything *except* the one needed thing? I do. I run around on an empty tank, using up all my energy and resources, wondering why I'm feeling drained—and suddenly I realize that my worship tank is empty. I have not been still. I have not been filled with God's presence. I have not *let go* and *let God*. Instead of praising and worshiping, I've been "worthlessing."

When we forget to stop and worship God—when we fail to do the one needed thing—it is like continuing to drive on a flat tire. It's like Martha running around her house like a chicken with its head cut off while the King of kings was in the living room, waiting. (See Luke 10:38–42).

We know that poor health choices lead to conditions which contribute to heart disease. Similarly, if we continue driving on the flat tire, allowing the world and its ways to push us on rather than stopping for a deep drink of living water, we cause more damage to our souls.

Bearing Fruit Requires Water

Worshiping our God is not just important—it's essential if we want to live, not only stress-free, but fruitfully. When we worship, He breathes into us, feeds us, and gives us living water. (See John 4:10). When we worship, we live.

If we want to be fruit trees, that is, if we want to bear fruit for God's kingdom, we must have water. Bearing fruit does not necessarily require more effort, more stress, more doing, on our part; it requires water:

> *"Blessed is the mana who walks not in the counsel of the wicked, nor stands in the way of sinners, nor sits in the seat of scoffers; ²but his delight is in the law of the LORD, ³He is like a tree planted by streams of water and its leaf does not wither. In all that he does, he prospers."*
> (Ps. 1:1-3, ESV)

The one needed thing is worship of the one true and everlasting God.

Rest for Our Souls

Christian philosopher Dallas Willard described the soul as the deepest level of life and power in the human being. He said that when our souls are filled with God, we are constantly refreshed and exuberant in all we do. Weariness is a sign of a soul not properly rooted in worship.[7]

We find rest for our souls when we are yoked with Jesus: *"Come to me, all you who are weary and burdened,"* He said, *"and I will give you rest. Take my yoke upon you and learn from me, for I am gentle and humble in heart, and you will find rest for your souls"* (Matt. 11:28–29). Now, *that's* stress relief!

The Shadow of Your Smile

One night, I was upstairs in my house, working in my office, when I heard my husband call to me from downstairs. I could faintly hear the sound of music coming from down there too, but I couldn't tell what it was. I told him I would come downstairs soon.

A few minutes later the music was louder, and again I heard him call to me to come downstairs. Again, I told him I would be there soon. Finally, the music was so loud I could hardly hear myself think, so I went downstairs. My husband was standing there in the middle of the room with the music playing, waiting to dance with me. On the stereo was the first song we had danced to at our wedding: "The Shadow of Your Smile."

He took me in his arms, and we danced and danced and danced.

Invitation to the Dance

Sometimes God calls out to us, His beloved, longing to be with us and invites us to dance. He wants to hold us, to lead, to enjoy our company, but we're too busy, too caught up in our own stuff, too *stressed*. We don't have time. Still, God does not give up. He doesn't walk away from the dance floor. He keeps calling. He is willing to invite us again and again and again. He wants nothing more for us than to come to Him and spend time with Him.

Worship is the main way we connect with our Creator. It is a place and a time and a frame of mind and heart. Worship is the place where we stop and reach out our arms and say, "*Yes, Lord, yes—let's dance. Please lead! Yes!*"

Worship is the time when we open our hands, let go of our stuff, let our hearts rest, and yoke ourselves to Him.

The Key to Worship

A. W. Tozer said that we were made to worship God: "God gave to man a harp and said 'Here above all the creatures that I have made and created I have given you the largest harp. I put more strings on your instrument, and I have given you a wider range than I have given to any other creature. You can worship me in a manner that no other creature can.'"[8]

Worship of God is what we were created for. When we worship anything or anyone else, we lose our identity, our purpose; life is meaningless. Our souls are left empty.

But worship is not for us; it is not a time set aside for us to get through our prayer lists. Worship is a time to honor God, to be still and know that He is the One and Only, to become more and more aware of His presence. We can approach Him on the basis of the mercy seat:

"Therefore, brothers, since we have confidence to enter the Most Holy Place by the blood of Jesus, by a new and living way opened for us through the curtain, that is his body, and since we have a great priest over the house of God, let us draw near to God with a sincere heart in full assurance of faith, having our hearts sprinkled to cleanse us from a guilty conscience and having our bodies washed with pure water." (Heb. 10:19–22)

Through His death on the cross, Jesus Christ made a way for us to worship and draw near to His Father. He became our High Priest. In the Old Testament, the High Priest offered sacrifices over and over again. On the cross, Jesus was the offered sacrifice, the lamb who was slain; and He once and for all made a way for us to enter into the very presence of God.

He made a way, and He is the way.

That is how we worship. That's the key: we are able to enter because Jesus made a way for us. Worship is for and about *Him*, not us.

David's Passion

King David was passionate about the presence of God. It was the one thing he lived for. *"One thing I ask of the Lord, this is what I seek; that I may dwell in the house of the Lord all the days of my life, to gaze upon the beauty of the Lord and to seek him in his temple."* (Ps. 27:4)

All David wanted to do—his driving ambition—was to worship God.

Can you imagine beginning every day with worship? Maybe you already do that. Think of it as tuning an instrument (you!) first thing in the morning so that you can play your worship song all day long—so that you can be your song. Then, whenever you hear Him say, *"Want to dance?"* you can enthusiastically respond, *"Yes!!"*

A day or two before Christmas last year, I was in the drugstore, and I heard a voice over the loudspeaker: "Are you stressed? Are you burned-out? Consider ways to rest, ways to alleviate anxiety during this season." The voice went on to suggest several strategies to relieve stress and anxiety--read a good book, take yoga, seek counseling. But the voice did not mention the one needed thing. It didn't mention dancing with God or even your spouse, for that matter.

The world offers all sorts of answers and strategies and solutions for filling our empty tanks, but the One who gives living water is the only source that satisfies.

It's time we deal a death blow to stress so that we can live fully into the promises of God, so that our hearts will beat again with His purposes. Exhausted, we lose our focus of worship, but God continues to draw us back. Jesus reminds us that only by remaining connected to the vine are we able to not simply reduce our stress symptoms but eliminate them. (See John 15:5-7).

What Worship Reveals

As he was trying to understand a God who apparently demanded worship, C. S. Lewis discovered something that radically changed his outlook: God communicates His presence through worship. Lewis came to recognize that it was when he worshiped—while he was authentically engaged in the worship process—that God revealed Himself: His thoughts, His ways, His truth, His rest.[9]

Who wouldn't want to know the thoughts of God? We all want to hear from Him, don't we? It is through worship that He reveals Himself.

Worship Is Being

Worship is not necessarily reading the Bible, although that is needed. It isn't necessarily praying either, although that is important. Worship is *being*. It is being with God . . . and being content to be there. Worship is sitting at His feet in the living room, like Mary. It is the one needed thing in a world filled with stress.

Enemy Opposition

The enemy will do all he can to keep us from worshiping God. He will encourage us to stay too busy, keep us distracted, or cause us to worship something or someone other than God. Satan tried to get Jesus to worship him. He promised Jesus the kingdoms of the world if He would worship him. (See Matt. 4:8–9). Satan knows that we will serve the one we worship. Think about that for a minute. Do you get that you may be worshiping something or someone other than God? The enemy will try to divert you to spend your time elsewhere; he will tempt you with doubt and unbelief; he will even suggest that your time is better spent doing something more worthwhile. But you see, he knows: he knows you will become like Jesus if you worship the Son of God—that you will be changed—and that is exactly what our enemy does not want!

Satan knows that worship precedes service, and if you worship God, you will also serve Him.

As I mentioned, I have a yearly ritual of spending time with the Lord, seeking His will for the New Year. One year, as I sought Him, the word the Lord gave me was *surrender*.

"Haven't I already done that?" I asked Him. "Don't I do that every day? Surrender. What is it about that word that I don't really understand?"

Let's take a look at how one man viewed surrender: the patriarch Abraham.

Surrender and Worship

Some time later God tested Abraham. He said to him, *"Abraham!"* *"Here I am," he replied. Then God said, "Take your son, your only son, whom you love—Isaac—and go to the region of Moriah. Sacrifice him there as a burnt offering on a mountain I will show you.* (Gen. 22:1–2)

Abraham could not comprehend with his intellect why God told him to sacrifice his son. Isaac was the son of the covenant, the one from whom the nation of Israel would be birthed, so killing Isaac made no sense whatsoever to Abraham. But he took his son to the mountain as God had instructed him, and he prepared to kill Isaac on the altar as an act of worship.

"Early the next morning Abraham got up and loaded his donkey. He took with him two of his servants and his son Isaac. When he had cut enough wood for the burnt offering, he set out for the place God had told him about. On the third day Abraham looked up and saw the place in the distance. He said to his servants, "Stay here with the donkey while I and the boy go over there. We will worship and then we will come back to you." (Gen. 22:3–5)

Once he surrendered, he could worship.

Abraham had to surrender his intellect on the way to Mount Moriah. At that moment, for what God wanted him to understand, Abraham's intellect would only have been a hindrance, not a help. No way could he have understood what God was asking him to do by thinking it through.

But one thing he did understand was worship. He prepared himself and his son to go to Mount Moriah to worship. He knew how to do that. And this time worship would require all. Abraham could not hold back anything, even his son.

He surrendered in worship, and God provided another sacrifice.

Okay, so that year my focus was surrender. But I have to admit to you that it sounded scary to me, particularly since I already thought I'd been there and done that. But God spoke . . . and now I had no choice. Like Abraham, I had to go to my own mountain. I didn't know where or what my Mount Moriah would be, but I committed to surrender.

Surrender, letting go and giving in, leads to worship; and worship engages our entire being. So I intend to worship my God at every opportunity, and expect that the Holy Spirit of God will show me what it is I must surrender.

Fully Surrendered?

If surrender and worship really are so deeply connected, then that begs a question: are you fully surrendered? That's the question of the day, the challenge we all face. Where and what is your Mount Moriah? What must be put on the altar as your act of worship? Your job? Your marriage?

What do you need to surrender to make more space for God?

Speaking of Surrender and Worship...

The king of Babylon had besieged Jerusalem, and Scripture tells us that the king of Judah was taken captive. Nebuchadnezzar, king of Babylon, ordered his officials to bring in some of the Israelite males who were bright and handsome and qualified to serve in the palace. The boys were given a daily amount of food and wine from the king's table and were to be trained for three years and after that enter the king's service. Daniel was among these young men.

One day the Babylonian administrators talked Nebuchadnezzar into issuing a decree stating that anyone who prayed to any foreign god, and not to Nebuchadnezzar himself, would be thrown into a very unique jail cell, a pit containing hungry lions. Well, Daniel had no intention of worshiping anyone but the one true God. He was surrendered to Him. And he continued to worship God three times a day.

Of course, when the Babylonian administrators found Daniel praying, they tossed him into the lions' den, expecting Daniel to be the lions' dinner that night.

Do you know the rest of the story? Actually, the king liked Daniel and was distraught at this turn of events. Nebuchadnezzar was sorry he had signed that decree into law. He said to Daniel, "May your god, whom you serve continually, rescue you!"

The king was so worried about Daniel that he couldn't sleep that night. And early the next morning, he called out to the young captive, "Daniel, servant of the living God, has your God, whom you serve continually, been able to rescue you from the lions?"

Daniel answered, "Long live the king! My God sent his angel to shut the lions' mouths so that they would not hurt me, for I have been found innocent in his sight. And I have not wronged you, Your Majesty."

The story goes on to say that the king "was overjoyed and ordered that Daniel be lifted from the den." Not a scratch was found on him. Why? Because "he had trusted in his God" (Dan. 6:6–23).

Daniel would not back down from worshiping His God. He let go and let God. Because he had surrendered and worshiped with his whole being, God delivered Him.

A Peek into Heaven

Scripture tells us that worship is the activity in which all lovers of God are engaged. Can you imagine? All day worshiping the One who sits on the throne? Let's peek into heaven for a moment and see what worship looks like there. Imagine that we are standing around the throne of God, joining the angels as they praise God:

> *After this I looked, and there before me was a door standing open in heaven. And the voice I had first heard speaking to me like a trumpet said, "Come up here, and I will show you what must take place after this." At once I was in the Spirit, and there before me was a throne in heaven with someone sitting on it. And the one who sat there had the appearance of jasper and carnelian. A rainbow that shone like an emerald encircled the throne. Surrounding the throne were twenty-four other thrones, and seated on them were twenty-four elders. They were dressed in white and had crowns of gold on their heads. . . . In the center, around the throne, were four living creatures. . . . Day and night, they never stop [worshiping].* (Rev. 4:1–4, 6, 8a

Go closer. Can you hear the sound of the living creatures, the elders and the angels worshiping?

*"'Holy, holy, holy is the Lord God Almighty,' who was, and is, and is to come."
Whenever the living creatures give glory, honor and thanks to him who
sits on the throne and who lives for ever and ever, the twenty-four elders fall
down before him who sits on the throne and worship him who lives for ever
and ever.* (vv. 8b–10)

I'm willing to bet there's no stress in *that* environment.

Do you believe that worshiping God and putting Him first in your life
will deliver you from the stress and trials you face? Well, it will. You may
have a lion prowling around, seeking to devour you, but God will deliver
you. He is faithful. He delivered me as an exhausted young mother living
in a foreign country. He transformed me from feeling depleted and being
irritable to being energized by the Holy Spirit and a joyful, peaceful wife
and mother.

Mary sat at the feet of Jesus and worshiped Him. Abraham worshiped
God in complete surrender and obedience on Mount Moriah, even though
God was asking him to do the unthinkable. Daniel would not stop worshiping His God, no matter what. They all knew that life flows like living
water from worshiping our Creator. Life begins and ends, ebbs and flows,
around His royal throne. And it is there—as we worship Him—that we
will find relief from our stress. Our spiritual hearts will be revived much
like a physical heart damaged by the effects of stress and healed by the
surgeon's hands.

Friends, as lovers of Christ, we have to make our way back to worship. Matt Redman wrote a song a few years back titled "The Heart of
Worship." My favorite lines go, "I'm coming back to the heart of worship /
And it's all about You / All about You, Jesus / I'm sorry, Lord, for the
thing I've made it . . ."[10]

If we are going to deal with our stress, we need to come back to the
heart of worship—worshiping God alone, not our jobs, our relationships,
our possessions. All focus must be on Jesus.

Be still and know that He is God. He loves you and wants to free you from your stress. He will never forsake you, and that's cause for worship. So worship Him. Praise Him. He *inhabits* your praises. (See Ps. 22:3 KJV).

And know that He will reveal Himself to you when you accept His invitation to the dance.

Jesus is fully able to deal with our stress. Here's His word for you today:

"I have said these things to you, that in me you may have peace. In the world you will have tribulation. But take heart; I have overcome the world."
(John 16:33 ESV)

CHAPTER 5

Three Deadly Ds: Doubt, Discouragement, and Disappointment

Friends, it's time to tell your heart to beat again. But
doubt, discouragement, and disappointment are three
thieves who sneak in the back door of our lives and cause
us to flat line. In a moment we are going to take a look at
how each of these deadly d's robs us of peace, rest, and
contentment in Christ. But for now, enter with me into
the scene with Martha and Mary

(LUKE 10:38–42).

MARY WAS SITTING at the feet of Jesus. She only had eyes for him. Martha
was busy in the kitchen. Mary was getting fueled for the busy life that she
faced, and there is no telling what storms were brewing in her life. But
she chose to sit. She chose to believe and not doubt that Jesus was all she
needed. She somehow knew that all of her life's disappointments could be
dealt with by sitting at Jesus' feet.

Mary probably had a lot of storms in her life. We don't know for sure,
but we do know that no one is exempt from storms—those things in our
lives that wreak havoc.

Perhaps as she sat at the feet of Jesus, she was experiencing one. But you
can be sure of one thing: When she sat at Jesus' feet, her storm was stilled.

Perhaps the storm was within her own soul. You know, the kind where you feel battered, wounded, depressed? My guess is that the longer she remained at Jesus' feet, the more the waves of peace washed over her weary soul. Perhaps she was a people pleaser, longing to be set free and just be herself. As she sat at His feet, even the hurricane wrath of her irritated sister drove all the people pleaser right out of her. She simply wasn't going to get up and help in the kitchen. She preferred to sit in the peace waves.

Doubt, disappointment, and discouragement often go hand in hand. Trusting in God's love and care for us helps us deal with these three deadly Ds. The apostle Peter knew firsthand how this trifecta could impact lives because he dealt with them on a regular basis.

The story about Jesus walking on the water, in John 14, really fits here. What a great storm story it is, always worth rereading and reimagining.

Jesus had taken a boat to a solitary place, but crowds had followed him, so he ministered to them. Jesus then told the disciples to take the boat and go on ahead of Him to the other side of the lake while He dismissed the crowd. After He released the people who had come to hear Him teach, He went up on the mountain to pray. He needed to be renewed, refueled. (Guess who took Jesus by the hand as He made His way up the mountainside).

When evening came, the disciples' boat was at a distance from land, and the waves began to swell. The boat was tossed, and in the fourth watch of the night, Jesus went out to them, walking on the lake. The disciples were terrified and at first thought He was a ghost. But Jesus saw their fear and told them to have courage.

Peter, our impetuous friend, jumped out of the boat and began to walk on the water toward his Lord. But when Peter saw the wind-whipped waves, he was afraid; he took his eyes off Jesus, and he began to sink.

Like it or not, aren't we so like Peter? The storm is raging around us-- our marriages are falling apart; our kids are rebellious, on drugs, unwilling to talk to us; our finances are a mess—and then we see God. At least, we hope it is Him. It could be a ghost; it could be wishful thinking. But we grab the life preserver, clinging to Him, because when we are faced with the towering eye wall, the most devastating part of the storm, God is our only hope. You see, Jesus Himself is the eye of any storm of doubt or discouragement we hit. He is our safe tower. I love the deep mystery and irony of God in this. He loves us, and He is Love; He leads us to the eye of the storm, and He is the eye; He will give us peace as He leads us through the storm, and He is the peace.

The enemy's mission is to kill, steal, and destroy, specifically to destroy our hope and trust in God. But Jesus' mission is to set the captive free from discouragement, disappointment, and doubt. The Bible offers many examples of ordinary men and women who clung to Him in the midst of the storms of discouragement in their lives. Again and again we are shown how people like you and me found God and entered the eye of the storm that threatened to overtake them.

Trust Is the Key

When ordinary, everyday people trust God through their responses to the storms of life, they become extraordinary.

We may not like it much, but we do know that storms of doubt are inevitable. And it is our response to them that determines whether we

- become bitter, or better
- simply weather the storm, or become storm warriors
- give up and let the storm beat us up, or surrender to God and allow Him to lead us up the mountainside, over the boulders
- run around like frantic chickens, or soar like eagles and allow the storm to take us to the eye of His presence

Job the Storm Survivor

Who had as many storms in his life as Job? Can you imagine? This man full of faith lost his children, his home, and his livestock; then he suffered horribly painful lesions and boils all over his body; and finally, even his friends and wife turned on him. Amidst all of this—not just one hurricane but one after another, storm upon storm—Job responded by trusting God. He did not understand any of it, couldn't fathom why a loving Father would allow such an overwhelming eye-wall onslaught. Job had a million questions and not one answer. But in spite of it all, contrary to the world's counsel, Job's response was: *"Though he slay me, yet will I hope in him"* (Job 13:15). How was he able to say that? "He knows the way that I take," Job declared, concluding, *"When he has tested me, I will come forth as gold."* (23:10)

With the storms raging around him, and his own wife telling him that death would be better (2:9), Job bet on God. He trusted that God was as good as His word. And it paid off.

David the Storm-Slayer

How about the boy who killed the giant with one stone? Anointed to be king of Israel, David ran head-on into a storm named Saul. King Saul, the first and current king of Israel, was jealous of David and relentlessly pursued him. He was obsessed with killing young David. In the midst of it all—running from the king and his army, hiding in caves, fearing for his life—David trusted God. He knew his time to be king would come, and he knew it beyond the shadow of a doubt because the true King of Israel, the eternal King, had told him so. God was David's place of refuge in the middle of Hurricane Saul.

When David was hiding from King Saul in a cave at Engedi, he had a great opportunity to surprise Saul and be rid of him for good, but he chose not to. It was not time.

David bet on God's timing and authority. And it paid off.

Mary's Storm

Mary the mother of Jesus hit an eye wall when the angel of the Lord told her she would become pregnant. When the angel informed this small town teenager that she would be the mother of the Savior of the world, do you think that was part of her plan? Do you think she thought it was a good plan? Do you think Mary thought she was *right for the job*? She was engaged to Joseph and an out of wedlock pregnancy would be a profound disgrace. Worse, the Jewish religious laws at that time dictated that a woman pregnant out of wedlock should be taken to the edge of town and stoned to death.

How could Mary explain this to Joseph? How could she make him believe her story? She almost couldn't believe it herself. "Uh . . . the Holy Spirit impregnated me—I've never had a physical relationship with any-one! Honest! I don't exactly understand it either . . . but it's true. Really. The King of the universe has asked me to give birth to His Son. I promise."

Fat chance Joseph or anyone, including Mary's parents, friends, and family, would believe that story. Would you?

If God had not spoken to Joseph in a dream, it would have been a huge, tragic mess. No way could Mary have convinced her fiancé that she was a "handmaid of the Lord," chosen by God Himself (Luke 1:38 KJV).

But Mary opted to trust God. He had handpicked her, and she said yes. Where could she go to flee from His presence anyway? Nowhere— which is *now here* in one word. God is not only in the *now here*, He is also in the *back there* and the *up ahead*. He is anywhere and everywhere we are.

Mary bet on God's sovereignty and powers of persuasion, and it paid off.

Paul and Silas and a Jailhouse Storm

One day, in Philippi, Paul and Silas ended up in prison. (Actually, for Paul prison was like a home away from home). The story is found in Acts 16, and it is one of the Bible's most amazing, outlandish, crazy, fantastic stories about the eye of the storm. Paul had cast the devil out of a fortune-telling slave, and her owners, angry because their income source was dried up, dragged Paul and Silas before the magistrate in front of a crowd. Here's the rest of the story:

> The crowd joined in the attack against Paul and Silas, and the magistrates ordered them to be stripped and beaten. After they had been severely flogged, they were thrown into prison, and the jailer was commanded to guard them carefully. Upon receiving such orders, he put them in the inner cell and fastened their feet in the stocks.
>
> About midnight Paul and Silas were praying and singing hymns to God, and the other prisoners were listening to them. Suddenly there was such a violent earthquake that the foundations of the prison were shaken. At once all the prison doors flew open, and everyone's chains came loose. The jailer woke up, and when he saw the prison doors open, he drew his sword and was about to kill himself because he thought the prisoners had escaped. But Paul shouted, "Don't harm yourself! We are all here!"
>
> The jailer called for lights, rushed in and fell trembling before Paul and Silas. He then brought them out and asked, "Sirs, what must I do to be saved? (vv. 22–30)

How many people do you know who would sing in prison? At best they would fear being beaten up, right? But Paul and Silas didn't fear the beating because they had already been beaten to a bloody pulp *before* being thrown into prison.

How many people would stick around in prison once they had been released from their chains and their prison door "flew open?" A case can be made that when a miracle like that happens, you're supposed to take advantage of it, right?

Paul and Silas did not do what any sane person would expect them to do because they knew that they were meant to be exactly where they were. They were in the middle of this particular hurricane--and earthquake--because God intended for them to personally lead their fellow prisoners and their jailer to Him.

In the midst of the storm, Paul and Silas trusted God. The chains of fear and despair were broken as they praised Him, and their physical chains were removed when they stood their ground, resulting in the jailer and his family being saved. Paul and Silas bet on God's promise to set the captives free, and it paid off.

When we find ourselves in chains of bondage or despair or paralyzing fear or loneliness, if we trust and praise God, He will break the chains. The presence of God replaces the chains of whatever prison may contain us. The storm may still rage, but looking for Him, praising Him, and thanking Him in the midst of it will take us directly into the eye of the storm, the peace of His presence.

Elijah's Storm—Inside a Cave

Elijah was a nut case. He had just experienced an extraordinary encounter with God on Mount Carmel—and then promptly forgot it.

In 1 Kings 18, Elijah confronted 450 false prophets of Baal on the mountaintop and challenged them to call on their god to send fire on a sacrificed bull. Of course, the fire never came. After a ridiculous display of self-mutilation and incantations to their supposed god, the gang of false prophets gave up. Then Elijah called on the one true God; fire fell, and the offering was consumed.

But something happened after that mountaintop experience that made him run for his life out of fear. The wicked queen threatened his life, and Elijah stopped trusting the God who had just demonstrated that He was Lord of all the storms. Elijah ran, and when he could run no more, he hid in a cave. Naturally, God found him there.

Remember the one place we can we flee from His presence? Nowhere. God is anywhere we are; he is *now here.*

God told Elijah to get a grip, to remember what He had just done, and to get back in the eye of the storm, where safety was guaranteed.

As God met Elijah, He will meet you—anywhere, anytime, in the midst of any storm of doubt or discouragement you face. Even when you are a nut case. Even when you are doubtful or fearful. Even when it seems as though the waves will consume you.

Even when you find yourself in a cave.

God asks only that we trust Him to lead us through the storms and over the boulders. The place of immunity is the place of shelter in God. Once we find this place, nothing we encounter in life can defeat us. Not any storm. Not even death. The eye of the storm, God's presence, is the place where fear is replaced by His love, torment is replaced by His peace, Satan's lies are replaced by God's truth, and discouragement and despair are replaced with hope and faith.

All of us have doubts from time to time. We doubt we can finish a task that is too difficult. We doubt we can fix a broken relationship. We doubt we are smart enough, and the list goes on. Doubt can cause us to hold back from the call on our lives; it steals our joy and purpose and causes our spiritual hearts to weaken. Why? Because doubt is a destiny stealer, and the enemy knows that God has a purpose for each one of us. When we fully live into His purpose for our lives, we feel His pleasure; we know deep contentment; and we live contented lives. But if the enemy can get us to doubt, we lose out on all of it.

Let's start with a working definition of *doubt*. Doubt is a feeling of uncertainty or lack of conviction. *Conviction* is a firmly held belief or opinion. Putting this together paints the picture of a ship floating out to sea with no captain, no one to keep the ship on course. Without convictions, firmly held beliefs, we are like a ship floating aimlessly that may one day crash. We need an anchor.

Hebrews 6:18-20 says, *"Take hold of the hope set before us... We have this hope as an anchor for the soul, firm and secure. It enters the inner sanctuary behind the curtain, where our forerunner, Jesus, has entered on our behalf."* Our hope in Jesus, a firm anchor in any storm, pushes out doubt and uncertainty. Knowing that He went before us and made a way for us to enter into His presence, gives us confidence to press on.

In a world filled with no absolutes, people are floundering in search of a safe harbor, desperate for an anchor to keep their lives from floating aimlessly out to sea. Recently, I spoke with a young woman who has adopted a part of many religions. As if cherry picking, she chose the parts of each religion that seemed to fit her lifestyle. There were no absolutes, such as "Jesus is the only way to the Father," or "Jesus promises to be with you always," or "His Word is Truth—absolute truth." So she found herself drifting—drifting in her marriage and in her relationships, with no sense of purpose. And there are many like her who desperately need an anchor for their souls, but they doubt that Jesus is the one who can anchor them. Doubt is a dream killer.

In the wonderful book *The Dream Giver*, Ordinary, who wants to be a Somebody, sets off to pursue his dream. He leaves his familiar job, family, and friends, and steps out in faith.

But along the way he encounters his Mother, Uncle, and Best Friend, who try to persuade him to turn back. They block his view of the bridge that will take him to his dream. Ordinary begins to doubt his dream. He starts to question the risk he is taking.

Then Ordinary hears a voice calling his name. It is Champion, a Somebody from his hometown, who used to be a Nobody. Champion encourages Ordinary and gives him the courage to keep going, not doubting the call, but pressing on.[11]

Doubting that God is for us and not against us, doubting that we have a God-given purpose, doubting that our lives count for something—all of these can cause our spiritual hearts to faintly beat. It is only when we step out, trusting God and knowing that with Him all things are possible, that we can become champions for Christ, fully living into our purpose.

———

The next deadly "D" is discouragement. *Dis*-courage. Are you able to see what that word means? It means "to deprive of courage." Discouragement steals our courage. We lose perspective, hope, and joy. Our spiritual hearts take a hit. Discouragement is a tool in the hands of the enemy to get us off course and cause us harm. But God draws near to the faint of heart when we cry out to Him. Hear a cry from David's heart: *"Hear my cry, O God; give heed to my prayer. From the end of the earth I call to You when my heart is faint; lead me to the rock that is higher than I. For You have been a refuge for me, a tower of strength against the enemy"* (Ps. 61:1–4 NASB).

When my oldest daughter became a teenager, I was discouraged. She was a challenging, strong willed girl, and I felt like a failure as a mother. I sought the Lord, and He heard my cry. I turned to Him in desperation, and He drew near to me. Raising a strong willed child caused me to lean on the Lord and seek Him alone as my refuge. When you don't have an alternative, seeking God is a good plan.

Otherwise the ditch you are in gets deeper and more difficult to escape. I turned to Him in prayer. I began to devour scripture. I made space for God to lead and direct my path, and the most challenging time in my life became the sweetest. The Holy Spirit was transforming me and turning my discouragement into courage. I found strength in His arms.

So, all you wonderful mothers out there, don't waste time on guilt or feelings of failure. Turn to the Lord, and He will use this time in the wilderness for your good. And when you come out of the desert, you will have a newfound strength that can stand against discouragement. And it will. Again and again, discouragement will wiggle its way into your life. But each time you allow the Lord to turn it for good by drawing near to Him, strength will arise within and discouragement will be defeated.

The third deadly "D" is disappointment. Notice anything about this word? Dis- appointment. When we fall prey to disappointment—and we all do from time to time—we miss our *divine* appointment. Let me explain.

When we are disappointed, we look down. We end up, as King David might put it, in "the pit." (See Ps. 57:6; 88:6). But God specializes in reaching down to our pit and pulling us out when we turn to Him. He washes us clean with His Word and delivers us from our pain. Our part is to cry out for help.

King David describes this beautifully: "He drew me up from the pit of destruction, out of the miry bog, and set my feet upon a rock, making my steps secure" (Ps. 40:2 ESV).

The remarkable thing about pit living is that God finds us there. There is no place we can hide from Him. And when He finds us, we encounter Him in ways we had never imagined. The pit has a way of transforming us. If we look up to God, we experience a divine appointment with Him in which He changes our perspective, gives us hope, and causes our hearts to beat again. When we look down, however, we lose perspective, become hopeless, and miss a God encounter.

I love God encounters. I look for them as I read through the Bible, and there are so many amazing stories of disappointed men and women in Scripture who needed God. Their lives were hanging in the balance, and they questioned, "Is God for me or against me?" Let's be honest. We find ourselves in that place all too often. Disappointment creeps in; questions consume us, but God never forsakes us.

Think about Moses. Although Scripture does not say that Moses was disappointed that He could not go into the promised land, you can bet he was. I realize that it was his fault due to disobedience; nevertheless, it hardly seems fair. He had spent a great portion of his life seeking to enter the promised land.

But God turned Moses' disappointment to a divine appointment. He told him that although he would not enter, His people would, and that every promise made to Moses would be fulfilled. He showed Moses the bigger picture. And I believe that when Moses went to be with the Lord, the Lord welcomed Him with open arms, saying, "Well done, good and faithful servant."

The three deadly D's threaten to flat line our spiritual lives. When any of these three press in, God, who never forsakes, will hear your cry. Seek Him. He will revive you once again. Have you grown weary and disappointed? Are you besieged by storm waves of discouragement and hurricanes of doubt? Find your place of rest in God. Make space for His Presence. He waits patiently to take you into the eye of the storm, that is His presence. Be bold and cry out to Him, and when He extends His hand, take it and follow Him. And tell your heart to beat again.

PART II

Rise Up—Reposition

CHAPTER 6

The Glory of God is Man Fully Alive

AT THIS POINT we have learned that the church, once asleep, is awakening. We are letting go of the old, giving our stress to God, and dealing death-blows to doubt, discouragement, and disappointment—those deadly Ds. Our spiritual hearts are abiding in God's presence. He has knocked, and we have let Him in, to dine with us. He has set before us a glorious banqueting table of His promises—truly a feast—and as we, the church triumphant, continue to seek His company, our hearts are being resuscitated. We are now poised to allow the Holy Spirit to reposition our lives for His purposes. No longer will we live life aimlessly, but victoriously and with purpose, taking back the land that we once lost. When we accept Jesus, our lives receive the light of new life in Him. As glory bearers, made in His image, we have the delight of participating with His work on earth so that God is glorified.

In the last quarter of the first century, Irenaeus, Bishop of Lyons in what is now France, wrote, "The glory of God is man fully alive."[12] Fully alive how? I'm sure he meant fully alive in *Christ*. It is Christ who gives us life in Him and calls us out to a world that has need of Him. Once alive in Christ, we glorify Him in the places to which He leads us.

For years I remember thinking, *"What is my purpose?"* I asked people and sought the Lord, but I still had no answer. One day, I heard His still, small voice: "Joanne, your call is to worship Me in everything you do."

Not that I was looking for some big platform, but somehow His answer did not seem so glamorous. Hollywood has deceived us into thinking we have to *do* something big, *be* something bigger, and then our lives are worth something. Our purpose is to love and honor God. We can start there. As we begin to do that, we will find our places of interest and our gifts to love and honor Him. Jesus was pretty clear about this: *"But seek first the kingdom of God and his righteousness, and all these things will be added to you"* (Matt. 6:33 ESV).

To be fully alive is to have Jesus living within us. I marvel that the Lord chose to set up house in us, that the King of glory would find us as His suitable dwelling place. And I have discovered that He is not interested in just being a visitor. He wants to inhabit our dwelling place. We are *His temples*! Paul wrote, *"Do you not know that you are God's temple and that God's Spirit dwells in you?"* (1 Cor. 3:16 ESV). And if that is not enough, listen to what Jesus says: *"If you abide in me, and my words abide in you, ask whatever you wish, and it will be done for you"* (John 15:7 ESV). In other words, when we reposition ourselves in Him and let His Word dwell in us, we have the privilege of asking Him to meet our needs!

Now, before you get anxious thinking about all of the unanswered prayers you have prayed, remember that Jesus knows best. He sees the big picture. He knows the greater yes. We are His beloved, and He longs to give us the desires of our hearts, but He is more interested in our being fully alive in Him than in giving us everything we ask for. His purpose— and ours—is to bring God glory. We are His image bearers, and we are called to impact our world with the light of Christ.

Christ in Us Transforms What's Around Us

When a living, breathing, walking, talking, Christ-loving Christian enters a room, the atmosphere in the room should change. Did you know that? *Your* presence, as a Christian with God's glory living in you, should transform the environment. If that sounds radical to you, it should. It is radical. And it is absolutely true. If the King of glory lives in you, then His presence, and an open invitation to His feast, goes wherever you go.

The more you yield to Jesus' life *in* you, and the more interior space you make available to Him, the greater the impact you will have wherever He plants you—in your family, on the job, in church, in missions, in relationships. Know why? Because if you allow less space for yourself and more for Him, it will mean more power, more love, more anointing in your life, and more of God's influence in everything you do and say. We all want that, don't we?

Or Do We?

Allowing more of God in our lives, and accepting and extending the invitation to His feast, means making space for Him by tossing out the stuff of ours that gets in the way, giving up control, turning the management of our lives over to the King. To us skeptical humans it seems better to be in charge, doesn't it? It is much less scary to be strong and independent and free thinking than it is to be weak and dependent and focused on an invisible God. Weakness is scary, right?

But the ways of God and His kingdom are radically different from our ways and the ways of the world in which we live. The kingdom of God and the kingdom of us could not be more dissimilar.

But giving up control is easy! . . . Just kidding! Giving up control is hard. Anyone who has tried it knows just how difficult it can be. But what if you discovered that you, filled with His Holy Spirit, could change the atmosphere in a room? What if each time you offered an invitation to the King's feast, someone accepted? Would that be worth giving up control of your life to the King?

If your family life changes because of the amazing influence of God in you, if your coworkers are transformed by who they see living in you, and if all your relationships take on new and deepened meaning because you carry the King's glory, then hasn't giving up control to Him been worth it? Do you have a better plan and a greater adventure than that in mind? It can happen, because you are a glory carrier. It's true. Don't you think it is a more than fair exchange, His life for yours?

Jesus said, *"Whoever would save his life will lose it, but whoever loses his life for my sake will find it"* (Matt. 16:25 ESV). I would rather take on Jesus' life and invite Him to live in me than live without Him. He is the only One who can reposition us and empower us to make a difference in the world.

Called to Shine

You are called to shine in a dark world, and that requires making space for the lamp and the light of Christ in your life. Jesus said, *"You are the light of the world. A town on a hill cannot be hidden. Neither do people light a lamp and put it under a bowl. Instead they put it on a stand and it gives light to everyone in the house"* (Matt. 5:14–15).

Where do you need to shine? With whom do you need to share the light? To whom do you need to extend an engraved invitation to God's feast?

A Breathtaking Mystery: We in Him, He in Us

Paul said that in God we live and move and have our being (Acts 17:28). And—what a wonderful mystery!—He wants to dwell in us—in every corner of our lives. Again, He doesn't just want to visit us every now and then; He wants to inhabit us and make our hearts His dwelling place. And we must consciously, intentionally make room for Him.

Think of the rooms in your house. Are those in which you spend a lot of time cluttered with furniture or accumulated junk you've collected over your lifetime? Stuffed with your stuff? Is there room enough for you to sit down and enjoy the room and for others to sit down with you?

Now think about your spiritual house. What does God find when He comes in? Does He find the living room cluttered with your stuff? Or is He able to move freely? Is there space enough for all He wants to do in you?

Preparing the room is the key if you want to make space for Him, if you want Him to fill you, if you want Him to overflow your heart with His glory.

The House That Solomon Built

Solomon's father, David, had it in his heart to build a temple, but God told David that Solomon would build it instead. After David got over his initial disappointment, he rolled up his sleeves and set out to help his son build. David invested in the temple before he died, and Solomon completed it. According to Scripture, the glory of God filled the space: *"When the priests withdrew from the Holy Place, the cloud filled the temple of the LORD. And the priests could not perform their service because of the cloud, for the glory of the LORD filled the temple"* (1 Kings 8:10–11).

Today, you are the temple; God resides in you! That was His plan from the start. And when His glory fills His temple, you, all the doing and all the striving and all the activity cease. He takes over. His life for your life. The feast is ready now. The table is set. You are invited.

What Is in You?

Nehemiah was a man of God who was called away from Babylon to help rebuild Jerusalem's broken-down wall. He completed his assignment and returned to Babylon, but then Tobiah, an avowed enemy of God's people, filled God's temple with his own household goods. Here is how Nehemiah responded:

> *Some time later I asked [the king's] permission and came back to Jerusalem. Here I learned about the evil thing Eliashib had done in providing Tobiah a room in the courts of the house of God. I was greatly displeased and threw all of Tobiah's household goods out of the room. I gave orders to purify the rooms, and then I put back in them the equipment of the house of God with the grain offerings and the incense.* (Neh. 13:6–9)

Nehemiah cleaned out God's house and filled it with God's things.

What is in your temple? More accurately, what is in you? Are there things in you that need to be removed so that the God who wants to dwell in the center of your soul can live, move, and have His being in you? What needs to be repositioned or purified so that you can make more space for God?

It is simple but not easy. To partake of the feast of God's presence, we must remove what is not of Him and fill the resulting available space with more of Him.

As God's glory fills us, we suddenly realize that we are, at last, fully alive! Our hearts begin to beat with a new and glorious sound, loud and strong, and the glory of God shines through us. We are His glory carriers! Sometimes, however, we simply do not feel like glory carriers. We feel like earthbound people with lead feet and empty hearts.

A few years ago, I found myself in a rut, going through the motions of living out my life by rote. Have you been there? Sometimes we simply get stuck doing the same things, the same way, without checking in with the Lord to see if He wants to shake things up a bit. Part of the issue is dullness of heart. The only way to stay connected to the Shepherd's voice is to *make time to hear it.* Jesus was clear that we, His sheep, can hear His voice (John 10:27). But our busy lives crowd Him out. He is talking, but we have not been listening. I liken it to having our spiritual antennae down. So this was a season in my life where I found myself not tuning in, not seeking God with my whole heart, soul, strength, mind. My prayer life and devotions were lifeless. The Word, of course, was not lifeless; it is *a living Word.* But my heart had become dull of hearing.

Then I came across the quote by Irenaeus—"The glory of God is man fully alive"—and I recognized that it was time to reposition my life for kingdom living. So I sought the Lord, asking Him why life had become rote and step-by-step, and He led me back to green pastures and restoration of soul. He led me away from the pasture where I had been grazing that was not green—that had become tasteless and lifeless.

You see, sometimes we simply get stuck. We know something is off, but we don't know how to get out of the rut.

In *A Shepherd Looks at Psalm 23*, the author describes sheep who have fallen into a rut. If they end up on their backs so that their feet can no longer touch the ground, they are trapped. If they stay there too long, their abdomens will fill with gas, and they will not be able to turn themselves over. Eventually they will die. The shepherd must go find the lost sheep and pull them out of the rut before they die.[13]

The Good Shepherd, Jesus Christ, also searches for His sheep who have lost their way. We are His sheep, and when He finds us flat on our backs in a rut, He comes and repositions us so that life and health are restored.

Friends, each of us has found ourselves in a rut at one time or another. Perhaps that is where you are now. Cry out to the Lord. You do not have to wave your hands and make a commotion so that He will see you are in trouble. You simply need to ask Him to help. You and I are often helpless when we get so low we cannot get up. The Good Shepherd will lift you out of the pit and reposition you on dry land.

Shepherds go before their sheep to check out the best grazing land, known as the mesa, and lead them there. Jesus, our Shepherd, does the same. He leads us beside still waters to grassy pastures and restores our broken souls. In that place of restoration, we are fully alive in the purposes of God and repositioned for life in His kingdom. Once there, we can rise up in our new position of strength.

The LORD is my shepherd; I shall not want.
He makes me lie down in green pastures.
He leads me beside still waters. He restores my soul.
He leads me in paths of righteousness for his name's sake. (Ps. 23:1–3 ESV)

Getting back to my story, I cried out to the Lord in prayer, knowing that I had spent enough time in the pit and it hadn't been much fun. Together, we made some life changes. I adjusted my schedule to make more space for God and to ensure that I was doing not just good things, but the best things—those things I was called to do. (We will look at this at length in chapter 8.). I made time to read, eat a healthier diet, and get more exercise and sleep. I made space for my family and friends. A few adjustments here and there repositioned me to work from a place of rest and strength in Christ.

Some of you reading this need to make some life adjustments too. Let the Lord lead you out of (whatever your rut you are in) and into green pastures so that you can be fully alive. Then the glory of God will shine out from within you, revealing Christ to a world desperately wanting their dead hearts to beat again.

CHAPTER 7

Repositioned for Destiny

EACH OF US is unique. That means you too. The God of all creation formed and fashioned you. Isn't that astonishing? You are one of a kind: there has been, is, and will be *no other exactly like you*, ever. You are like a snowflake, except much, much better; you were made to last . . . forever. And you were made for a purpose.

When our spiritual hearts beat with our God-given purpose, we are positioned to be game changers. Together with other unique world changers, we can impact our culture. In a world that is in need of a Savior, we believers *can* make a difference. We dare not hide the light of Christ within us. It's time for us to recognize our uniqueness and be salt and light to the lost. Jesus said:

> *"You are the salt of the earth, but if salt has lost its taste, how shall its saltiness be restored? It is no longer good for anything except to be thrown out and trampled under people's feet.*
>
> *You are the light of the world. A city set on a hill cannot be hidden. Nor do people light a lamp and put it under a basket, but on a stand, and it gives light to all in the house. In the same way, let your light shine before others, so that they may see your good works and give glory to your Father who is in heaven."* (Matt. 5:13–16 ESV)

Knitted by the Original Knitter

In awe of his Creator, David wrote, *"You knit me together in my mother's womb"* (Ps. 139:13). You, too, were "knit" in your mother's womb — with a purpose and destiny for your life.

I just watched a video to see how complicated the process of knitting is. Wow! To all you knitters, I am very impressed. The knit and purl stitches seem so intricate, yet the expert giving the demonstration made it look so easy.

That is how God, our Creator, intricately knit you in your mother's womb, one stitch at a time: knit, purl . . . knit, purl . . . knit, purl . . . you! When the Original Knitter planned your birth, He must have had a twinkle in his eye. *Ah, yes . . . this one will be one of a kind, exceptional, called and prepared for the work I have for her.* Because God has a special task for each of us. It is what we were made for: *"For we are God's workmanship,"* Paul wrote, *"created in Christ Jesus to do good works, which God prepared in advance for us to do."* (Eph. 2:10)

A Purpose Only You Can Fulfill

So, God created you with a purpose in mind; a purpose only you can fulfill. You and you alone. I do not mean by *yourself*, of course. I mean with God, by God, and through God. The point is, you have a purpose.

We are not meant to be wandering aimlessly around, wondering what our purpose is or what purpose there is to living. We will find our purpose by seeking Our Creator. When we know Him, He shares His secrets with us. He deposits His vision for each of us deep within our hearts — a vision that we alone can accomplish. Imagine with me . . . . God knowing you *before* you were made, having formed you whole in His mind before the knitting had even begun, then knitting you in your mother's womb. Now imagine with me for a moment God speaking to you about the destiny stirring your heart — a destiny that brings you fully alive in Him and fulfills the purposes of His heart. Imagine having *one* heartbeat with Him.

He leans down and whispers to you—into your ear and your heart and your soul, into your very blood and bones—the vision He has for your life. And He plants the seed of that vision deep in the soil of your being.

Imagine His inner dialogue: *Let's see . . . What color shall I make your eyes: brown like your mother's, or blue like your dad's? I'll make them blue. Now, let Me put in your genetic code and stitch in beautiful skin and curly hair and the slender fingers of a pianist. And your destiny . . . yes: I can see your destiny. Now let's plant the seed. I can't wait for you to be born so that you can walk with Me and relate to me even as My one and only Son Jesus does.*

See, God longs for you to walk with Him, but the choice is up to you.

"Your Free Will Is My Will"

I used to wonder why God would give us free will. Wouldn't it have been easier if we, His design, would be more like robots, loving him and obeying Him completely? As I have grown in my faith journey with Christ, I realize that He designed us this way so that we would be kingdom partners, having the ability to choose to love and be loved by Him, and to serve Him allowing His Holy Spirit to guide our steps. We can choose to walk away from His promises, but He never stops loving us and never stops pursuing us. We have no excuse concerning the fulfillment of our destiny, though we may try to find one. Moses did. He gave God a difficult time when he was called to lead the Israelites out of Egypt. Moses wondered how in the world he could lead a nation when he had difficulty speaking. Moses did not realize that God had given him everything he needed to accomplish his purposes. Ultimately, God's dream became Moses' dream to see God's people led out of captivity. Moses learned to trust that indeed God would supply his every need. Friends, you are uniquely set apart as God's own, created for His purposes. You have the ability and talent to do great things as you surrender to the Lord. You are His masterpiece; and as you seek Him, He will guide you in the use of your God given talents and purpose. He is your biggest fan, guiding you by His Holy Spirit, never leaving you, coaching you along the way.

That's great news, isn't it?

Living into Your Destiny: Finding Your Wings, Planting Your Seeds

In his song *"Find Your Wings,"* Mark Harris beautifully describes the challenge of living into our God-knitted destiny:

> I pray that God would fill your heart with dreams And that faith gives you the courage
> To dare to do great things. . . .
>
> It's not living if you don't reach for the sky I'll have tears as you take off
> But I'll cheer you as you fly. [14]

My son-in-law Gregg is a hopeless romantic, or, more accurately, a hope-*ful* romantic—there is nothing hopeless about him. For example, when he proposed to my daughter, Gregg rode up to our house on a horse, holding one hundred roses in his arms. He was also wearing armor, a helmet (visor up), a sheathed sword, a shield, and chain-mail gloves. He looked as if he had just finished a jousting tournament. Now, you have to understand that Gregg is not a proficient horseman, so his approach—on horseback, with an armful of roses—was risky from the start. I honestly don't remember if he was holding on to the reins at all. But Gregg was undaunted. He was on a mission of love. Sir Galahad had nothing on my future son-in-law.

Well, he dismounted his gallant steed, dropped to one knee, and proposed to my daughter. And she said yes. Wouldn't you?

I have told this story countless times, and every time I relate it, the women who hear it sigh . . . and the men most often look a little disgusted. After all, it makes them look bad. Who could ever measure up to that?

Funny thing is, it got to be a thing with the men in my life. My other son-in-law planned a romantic surprise dinner out on the dock behind our house, complete with music and white wedding bell decorations. And my son planned an elaborate proposal that included hundreds of candles and rose petals leading the way to the engagement ring.

Gregg didn't stop with his romantic ventures. The following spring he planted rye on the overpasses of our city in such a way that when winter came and everything else was dead, the hardy rye remained and said, *I love my wife.*

God plants His seed in your heart. It's a seed He designed with you in mind, and it says, "I love you . . . and I have great plans for you." When that seed is watered, it will begin to reveal the Father's heart for you, His vision.

Each of us is uniquely able to fulfill His dream. He made us that way.

Jeremiah's Call

In the thirteenth year of the reign of Josiah, the king of Judah, God spoke to Jeremiah: *"Before I formed you in the womb I knew you,"* He said. *"Before you were born I set you apart; I appointed you as a prophet to the nations."* (Jer. 1:5)

Now, Jeremiah wasn't so sure about this call "to the nations." He told God that he really wasn't a good speaker and that he was only a child. The Lord responded:

"Do not say 'I am only a child'. You must go to everyone I send you to and say whatever I command you. Do not be afraid of them, for I am with you, and will rescue you" (vv. 6–8).

I guess God had heard Jeremiah's brand of excuses a lot—the I-am-scared-to-death-of-the-call kind of excuses. He was ready with His answer to Jeremiah. He would be with him and rescue him when "mission impossible" seemed overwhelming.

Everyone has a dream planted deep within, and the fulfillment of that dream is our destiny. God created us to be dreamers and to co-labor with Him to see that the dream comes true.

Joseph's Dream . . . and Ours

Joseph had a dream that seemed a bit far-out. He dreamed that he was in the fields with his brothers, binding sheaves of grain, when all of a sudden his sheaf rose and stood upright. All his brothers' sheaves gathered around Joseph's sheaf and bowed down to it. Wow—pretty cool dream, Joseph. He thought so too, but he should have kept it to himself.

Joseph's brothers were already jealous of the preferential treatment their dad gave him — and now this? Did he think for a second they would ever be bowing down to him? His brothers were older than he, and they thought he was a spoiled, arrogant kid. They had had enough of the dreamer so they threw him into a pit, then sold him into slavery.

That happens now, too, doesn't it? Maybe not with quite as dire results, but we pridefully share our dreams, thinking that those with whom we share them are going to be happy for us — and we get thrown into the pit.

Mary had figured out the correct response to her dream. Remember? After the shepherds worshiped her son and the wise men visited, Mary simply pondered these things in her heart. Though her dream had been planted in her heart, her humility kept her dream in seed form, waiting for God's fulfillment. How wise for a small town, teenaged girl.

But Joseph got excited and shared his dream. Ponder? Young Joseph? Hardly. He was thrilled at the dream God had given him, but his pride landed him in the pit and in prison. He needed to develop the character of God, in order to fulfill his dream *God's* way.

Many of us have a great vision of what God is calling us to do, but, like Joseph, we get in the way of its fulfillment. So, the One who knit us in our mothers' wombs must allow a few trips to the pit to grow our character and to ensure that we will be prepared to carry out His call. "This is your dream, and you can fulfill it," He says, "but in My time."

God knows what He is doing.

Joseph's faith, integrity, and steadfastness eventually landed him in a position of influence in Egypt — second only to the Pharaoh himself — and in this position of authority and trust, he was able to save the nation of Israel and his entire family.

Seek the Dreamer

We are all given dreams. Each of us. In a wonderful variety of ways, God plants pictures in our hearts and minds of what He has called us to do. The moment He creates us, He envisions the works He has prepared for us. But if we are to fulfill His dream, we need to seek the Dreamer.

Some of us dream of being great athletes. Others dream of being successful businesspeople, mothers, fathers, artists, pastors, poets. What is your dream? Are you close enough to your Creator, and have you made enough space in your life to hear Him whisper: "This is the way; walk in it"? (See Isa. 30:21).

Sometimes on our path to achieve our destiny, we experience adversity. In Isaiah 30, God gave the Israelites a promise that although they had tasted affliction, His hand of mercy would guide them; He would show them the way. The Israelites, God's people, found themselves wavering between following the One true God and following other gods and their wavering caused them to lose their God given purpose as God's people.

Earlier in the passage (v.15), Isaiah reminds the Israelites that God has shown them the path to safety but they chose not to follow it and refused to put confidence in Him. And yet time and time again, God extended His hand of mercy to them so that they could fulfill their purpose to love and serve Him. As we make space for God, He will show us our path that He has designed for us. Often our adversity is due to our unwillingness to listen. God, our Teacher, must discipline us to set us on the right course so we can fulfill our destiny and His dreams will become our dreams.

Friendship Enables Destiny: Abiding in the Vision Maker

Jesus told His disciples that if they stayed close to Him—really close, like a branch to the vine—they would bear fruit that was lasting. (See John 15:5). Our close and growing friendship with Jesus is what enables us to dream His dreams, those dreams He made for us, that only we can fulfill. We must abide in Him.

To abide means to *stay close, fixed,* or *attached,* to the Vine—Jesus. Then He, Dream Weaver, offers us the sap of life that will nourish us, and enable us to bring His dream—and ours—to fruition. The fruit we bear is dependent on our connection to the Vine. When we remove the excess junk from our lives and connect to the life source in Christ, creative ideas and energy flow.

God's plan and purpose on this earth is to expand His kingdom. And we are the agents He has appointed to fulfill His plan. It is imperative that we reposition ourselves as branches connected to the vine. Only in that position will we fulfill our destiny. It is only by staying fixed to Jesus that our hearts will beat with purpose.

Thy Kingdom Come

Jesus taught us to pray, *"Our Father in heaven, hallowed be your name, your kingdom come, your will be done on earth as it is in heaven."* (Matt. 6:9–10)

Jesus' destiny was to come to earth and make a way for us to return to the Father through the forgiveness of our sins. Our destiny is to advance His kingdom on earth by proclaiming the good news of Jesus Christ—that He came to set the captives (us) free. So when we pray for God's kingdom to come on earth, we are in essence praying that we will be faithful to follow God's plan of expanding His kingdom on earth. We are committing ourselves to being the hands and feet of Christ on earth, His ambassadors. That really puts this dream thing into perspective, don't you think?

We Are the Design

We are God's dreamers, dreaming His dreams as we draw close to Him. Each of us has a unique calling, a unique contribution in making our Lord's dream come true. Have you ever stopped to think of it that way? If God is going to accomplish His will on earth, we are the way He is going to do it. He is the way and the truth and the life . . . and we are His way on Earth. It is true that He could easily reach down and zap things to turn out the way He wants, but that is not His design. We are at the heart of the Creator's design.

We are His design.

But will you believe that—or listen to the enemy's lies?

Die to the Lie

If you are going to be successful in fulfilling your destiny, step one, as we have seen, is to abide in the Vine. Step two is allowing God to free you from the untruths that oppose His vision.

What lies have you believed that have caused you to turn back from your call? Which lies have threatened to kill your dream and derail your destiny?

Maybe you don't think you have the skill, the right degree, or any degree at all. Perhaps you think you don't have enough time or that you didn't hear God correctly. Perhaps no one believes that you can do it, and you are beginning to believe the same thing. Maybe you have been praying for a breakthrough for so long, with no apparent result, that you have given up. The enemy is determined that you join forces with him and agree with his lies. He doesn't want to see God's kingdom grow; and if you fulfill your God-given destiny, then it thwarts his purposes. So the enemy plants seeds of lies.

But God's truth always prevails. Always.

Weapons of the Wise

In *The Traveler's Gift* by Andy Andrews, David Ponder is a man who has given up on life. When David is given the opportunity to visit with the angel Gabriel, Gabriel asks him a telling question:

"What is the difference in people, David Ponder," the angel began, "when they hit despair? Why does one person take his own life while another moves to greatness?". . . .

David shrugged. "I don't know. Maybe it's a difference in circumstances."

"Circumstances are rulers of the weak," Gabriel said, "but they are weapons of the wise. Must you be bent and flayed by every situation you encounter?"[15]

Here is the key. Circumstances can be deceiving. In the face of them, we can be tempted to think that there's no way to reach our dreams. If we believe that lie, rather than God's promises, then our circumstances have ruled the day. We can leave our place of comfort, take a risk, and boldly pursue our dreams—but not if we fall for the enemy's lies. Then we are doomed to fail. Only when we trust the Dream Giver will we follow our dreams to their successful completion. Only then can we partner with God to see His kingdom established on the earth.

We must let our hearts beat with the purposes of God. If we each will do that, then, together with other believers fulfilling their God-given purpose, this will become our finest hour. Friends, we must re-position our thinking in order to reposition our actions. Our actions often follow our thought life. If we believe lies that oppose our God given dreams, we will never feel fully alive. Repositioning our thinking by believing God's promises in His Word, will enable us to step out in faith into the places in which we are called. Joshua had to reposition his thinking after his mentor and leader Moses died. It was his turn to step into God's promise; it was his time to fulfill the dream God deposited in his heart to lead the Israelites into the Promised Land. He was fearful. God spoke these words to help him move forward: *"Have I not commanded you? Be strong and courageous. Do not be afraid; do not be discouraged, for the LORD your God will be with you wherever you go."* (Joshua 1:9). We too must listen to the voice of God alone stepping out in faith believing that God goes before us.

CHAPTER 8

De-Clutter Your Life

NOW THAT WE have gotten out of our rut, we must be sure to de-clutter our lives or we could end up right back where we were. If we are truly going to reposition our lives for kingdom living, then we need to take a hard look at what we are doing with our lives. Remember the overloaded potato in my introduction? One of the issues we face is our need to de-clutter our lives. We must make space for God to be our first love, our first priority. We are too busy, stressed, always pressed for time. What has overtaken *your* life?

In my earlier analogy about the baked potato, I described how the baked potato has undergone a transformation. We used to eat baked potatoes with butter only, and then restaurants began to offer sour cream, cheese, chives and an endless list of things we can add to the potato. Before it is all over, the potato is hardly recognizable. Our Christian lives can become similar to the overloaded potato. If our lives are cluttered, we lose the authentic flavor of a believer much like the flavor of the potato can become lost in the overpowering combination of condiments.

I have been in ministry for many years, and the most common thing I see with women is over-commitment, chiefly because women multitask well. We are wired to handle many balls in the air. For example, many of us have jobs outside of the home that we juggle along with being a wife and a mother. We may have aging parents who require our attention, as well as the demands of managing a household. To further complicate our predicament, we are wired for intimacy; therefore, relationships are important to us. Keeping up with friends and family members can be difficult when coupled with the demands of life, leading to stress. Women, we do not have to be victims of over-commitment. Much of the time, it is the choices we make that cause stress. Obviously, there are times in our lives when we are simply in a stressful season and the responsibilities we have are unavoidable. But we do not have to stay in that place forever. We do not have to assume that this is the new normal. We are called to joyfully serve God and others from a place of deep rest, and sometimes we must be practical (and not overly spiritual) to accomplish this. Making space for God is our number one priority, but we must take a look at our overcommitted lives as well. One feeds into the other.

Years ago, I discovered a way to de-clutter my life. I have shared this with hundreds of women who have found it helpful. In a season of over commitment and high stress, I sought the Lord. I struggled to find space to have a quiet time—read scripture, pray—but often that was the one thing on my plate I thought I could eliminate some days. Just like exercising, it was something I needed to do and wanted to do, but the demand of the urgent got in the way.

One day, when I knew I was at my breaking point, I cried out to the Lord. "I am done!" I said. "There is only one of me to go around, and I am stretched so thin I can hardly recognize myself." Anyone else ever felt that way? That day I recall closing my eyes and with a deep sigh saying, "What can be done, Lord?"

That's when I saw a large plate.

Now, mind you, this was not with my natural eyes; it was with my *special forces* eyes—the eyes of faith. As I continued to pray about what I was seeing, I had a sense that God was telling me to look at the things on my plate. I had done that many times before to try and see what I could take off my plate, but with no success. I remember the feeling of helplessness as I realized there was nothing that I could realistically take off my plate.

But that day God was in charge. He wanted me to look at my life through *His lenses*. And I did, and all I could see was clutter everywhere. I knew that, with the Holy Spirit leading me, I would need to take the time to remove each thing from my plate, one by one, and hand it to the Lord.

It took me weeks to do this. Each of my responsibilities I took off my plate, until the last day. All that was left were my children and my husband.

"Surely You do not want me to take them off my plate," I said. "This can't be You!"

But, yes, even those closest to me were handed over to Him. And then I saw the most extraordinary thing (again with my *special forces* eyeglasses): a gold plate, totally empty, shining brightly. "What is that, Lord?" I asked.

"It represents Me," He replied, *"royalty, your King, your Savior—your friend."*

It was apparent that the Lord had taken me through a process of transferring everything off my plate into His hands so that I could see that all the clutter of my life had hidden my deepest need—the one needed thing—to have a relationship with Christ and for that to be the center of everything.

One by one over the next few weeks, the Holy Spirit led me to put back some of the things that were on my plate (yes, my kids and husband were the first to go back), and He told me to lay some things down, and never put them on my plate again. I was surprised at what stayed and what had to go, but this exercise, led by the Holy Spirit, showed me a new way of living, one in which God was in charge. He wanted me to do what was best, not what was simply good. Some things that had been on my plate had been there because I'd wanted to please someone, or to prove myself. Others had been there simply because they had *always* been. Never mind that they were sucking the life out of me. It was just the way it was.

Women, we do not have to live that way. God's way is different.

Jesus, our role model, walked the dusty streets of the Middle East for just three short years, but how he packed those years! He was always on the go, ministering, healing, delivering, teaching. What was His secret? He followed His Dad's instructions. He went to a place of solitude with Him and used His secret service eyes to only do what He saw the Father doing. He set aside time to be with His Dad, knowing that at the core of it all there was a gold plate, and only His Father could fill it with the things He was called to do. You can be sure there were others He could have healed, but He went by instructions of the Father. *Jesus was not held hostage by the demands of the world.*

Jesus really needed faster transportation. If He could have strapped on those tennis shoes with wheels, He could have zipped through his day a lot faster. Have you ever thought about all the walking He had to do in His sandals? I suspect they were pretty worn-out. Here's the thing though: I doubt He was running from place to place. He walked; He stopped and looked around; He had conversations with anyone who wanted to talk with Him; He had an ongoing conversation with His Dad, with His disciples. His days were full, but they were intentional and purposeful. The crowds were at one moment praising Him and the next moment cursing Him. The Pharisees were condemning Him, and some of the lepers he healed forgot to thank Him. But nothing kept Him from His purpose: to heal, to set the captives free, and to proclaim the good news. The demands of the world, the tyranny of the urgent, did not hold His heart captive. He was free to do what His Dad told Him to do, and there were always enough hours in the day to do what had to be done.

How About You?

Do you ever end your day saying, "I wish there were more hours in each day?" I have said that plenty of times. There never seems to be enough time. But on those days when I surrender my calendar and press on toward the goal of following God's plan, I have ample time to do what needs to be done. The problem is, the demand of the urgent often gets in the way. Good intentions give way to the squeaky wheel that demands the grease.

I have good news. There is another way to live. I can't say that I live this way every day but I have found the secret to keeping the tyranny of the urgent from disrupting God's plans. It is a scripture we looked at in chapter 2: "Be still and know that I am God" (Ps. 46:10).

So now, whenever I'm faced with an interruption in my day, I stop and ask God, "Is this interruption from You?" I take the time to pray and ask Him for assistance. Fast-lane mode doesn't afford me the time to stop. But seeking-God mode does.

Jesus Did What His Father Said

As I said earlier, Jesus did only what His Father told Him to do. He wasn't influenced by the crowds that came out to see Him, and His actions were not dependent on what others said about Him. He was neither a people pleaser nor a politician. Jesus did what His Dad told Him to, and He trusted His Father in heaven completely.

What if we lived our lives like that? Wouldn't it simplify things?

Life in the fast lane is often connected to how we want others to perceive us. It seems as though everyone wants to be perceived as busy. No one wants to be a slacker. But is "busy" really a badge we want to wear? What if, instead, our badge read: *Unabashed Follower of the One and Only God*? What would our lives look like if we did only what the Father told us to do? Isn't significant work better than busy work? The only way we will know what He's saying to us is if we spend time with Him, sitting at His feet like Mary, focused on the one needed thing.

I am convinced that life is not meant to be complicated—life in Christ, that is. Imagine with me for a moment. Jesus goes up to the mountainside to pray. He has left His disciples and the enormous crowds to have some "down time" with His Dad. Imagine Jesus saying, "Dad, this was a great day. The demoniac was delivered, the man at the Pool of Siloam was healed, and we had that wonderful meal You provided for the five thousand on the hillside." Or maybe He would tell His Dad how great it was to have the conversation at the well with the Samaritan woman. Then He might say, "Hey, Dad, what's on the schedule for tomorrow? No, never mind—surprise Me!"

Whatever He said, we know that Jesus only did His Father's will: "I tell you the truth," He said, "the Son can do nothing by himself; He can do only what He sees His Father doing, because whatever the Father does the Son also does. For the Father loves the Son and shows Him all he does" (John 5:19). That is the key to purposeful living: Slow down to spend time with the Lord. Just as the Father showed Jesus what to do, He will instruct us and guide us in what to do too.

Beloved women, it may be time for you to take a look at the "plate" of your life. De-clutter to remove the excess from your life. Through that process your life can be restored to what God has for you and no more. Remember the image of the overloaded potato: strip the potato down to the essential ingredients that enhance its flavor. This de-cluttering may be the most significant thing you will do in your life: Learn to find a rhythm of grace wherein the Holy Spirit can examine your life and lead you day by day to follow His lead.

CHAPTER 9

Determined to Press On

I REMEMBER MY Father describing the benefits of exercising. One of the benefits of exercise is that it keeps our hearts healthy. It helps our heart muscle to become more efficient and better able to pump blood throughout our bodies. Regular exercise helps our body tissues do a better job of pulling oxygen from our blood allowing our heart to work better under stress and keep us from getting winded during high intensity activities. In other words, we should exercise to stay heart healthy; and one of the benefits as well is increased energy. Our spiritual hearts need to have regular exercise as well. Meditating on Scripture and prayer provides the oxygen we need to keep us spiritually healthy and enable us to press on in our spiritual journey. We are, in fact, energized by exercising our spiritual muscle in these ways. Otherwise we grow weary. Life can throw so many hard balls at us that it is a struggle to keep pressing on.

The church is tired of pressing on, and so are we as individuals. Our only hope is to reposition our spiritual hearts to be connected to the Vine, Jesus, and receive the oxygen we need. As John Eldredge says in his book *Waking the Dead*, there is a war going on for our hearts,[16] and it's a bloody war looking to destroy the body of Christ.

But God, as the Commander in Chief, is leading a war to regain our hearts and our passion for Him. As the Bridegroom, He pursues His bride with fervor. The battle belongs to Him, and He has already declared victory on the cross. But we do face skirmishes along the way. They are from the enemy, and they are meant to discourage us, defeat us, and derail our ability to press on in our spiritual journey.

One of my favorite stories in the Bible is the one about Jehoshaphat, the faithful king of Israel who was faced with a fearful battle against the Moabites and the Ammonites. These enemies had come to wage war against God's covenant people. In his fear, Jehoshaphat turned to God. He called for a fast, and he prayed to the Lord before the people.

Then in the midst of the assembly the Spirit of the LORD came upon Jahaziel the son of Zechariah, the son of Benaiah, the son of Jeiel, the son of Mattaniah, the Levite of the sons of Asaph; and he said, *"Listen, all Judah and the inhabitants of Jerusalem and King Jehoshaphat: thus says the LORD to you, 'Do not fear or be dismayed because of this great multitude, for the battle is not yours but God's. Tomorrow go down against them. Behold, they will come up by the ascent of Ziz, and you will find them at the end of the valley in front of the wilderness of Jeruel'"* (2 Chron. 20:14–16 NASB).

Jehoshaphat had a choice. Fear could have driven him to surrender or to turn and run. But he chose to trust God and press on, and God Himself saved the day.

We face a different battle. The battle for our hearts is intended to cause us to lose hope and to diminish our passion for Christ, and the daily skirmishes we face have the potential to wear us out. We have a real enemy, and he has been around since the beginning of time. Jesus confronted him in the wilderness and stood His ground. But from the moment Jesus stretched out his arms on the cross and said, "It is finished," providing once and for all the atonement needed to save all mankind, the enemy of our souls has tried to distract us, to wear us down. We find ourselves focusing on the world, losing perspective, and forgetting that we are only traveling through this world on the way to our real home. We fix our eyes on what we can see, and our eyes of faith weaken.

But God in His infinite love pursues us, His bride. He calls us to come out of the wilderness energized and fully awakened to His love, just as

Jesus emerged from the wilderness after forty days, energized and ready to walk fully in His call as Savior. (See Luke 4). The church, emerging from the wilderness, is now leaning on her groom. A poignant picture of this can be seen in the story of the lovers in the Song of Solomon: *"Who is that coming up from the wilderness, leaning on her beloved?"* (Song 8:5).

It is God who leads us out of the wilderness, but it is the wilderness that causes His bride to surrender to Him alone. Every wilderness experience is designed and allowed by God to draw us near to Him. Though the enemy will surely meet us in the wilderness, just as Satan met Jesus during His wilderness experience, the experience is designed to turn us toward our Groom and to cause our hearts to beat with His love and purpose.

Pressing on in our spiritual journey requires persistence. It is easy to see the finish line and yet give up hope out of weariness. But when we keep our eyes on Jesus, He carries us over the finish line. We were not designed to run the race with a backpack on our backs. Neither were we designed to run the race aimlessly but with purpose and with the freedom that Christ gives. (See 1 Cor. 9:26).

Paul describes our spiritual journey as a race:

Do you not know that in a race all the runners run, but only one gets the prize? Run in such a way as to get the prize. . . . Brothers and sisters, I do not consider myself yet to have taken hold of it. But one thing I do: Forgetting what is behind and straining toward what is ahead, I press on toward the goal to win the prize for which God has called me heavenward in Christ Jesus. (1 Cor. 9:24; Phil. 3:13–14)

Like Paul, we too must run, forgetting what lies behind so that we can look ahead. But that backpack on our backs slows us down. Beloved friends, it's time to throw the backpack down at the foot of the cross.

I think it's time that we talk about our spiritual authority. The church has supernatural weapons of warfare. We do not fight battles the same way the world does. Paul also wrote about this subject:

"For though we walk in the flesh, we are not waging war according to the flesh. For the weapons of our warfare are not of the flesh but have divine power to destroy strongholds. We destroy arguments and every lofty opinion raised against the knowledge of God, and take every thought captive to obey Christ, being ready to punish every disobedience, when your obedience is complete." (2 Cor. 10:3–6 ESV)

Friends, God has given us a different kind of weapon—the divine power and authority of God. It's time for the church to reposition itself under God's authority. We are not fighting the battles. It is God who fights our battles. The church has become tired of fighting battles in our own power when we have at our disposal the power and authority of God. But walking in that power requires you to answer some questions:

Does the church today have less authority than the first-century church that Peter and Paul and the first Christians began to build? Does today's church—the living body of Christ here on Earth—have any authority at all? Were the miracles and astonishing supernatural movements of the Holy Spirit that were routine in the book of Acts simply interesting phenomena for that time or legends from the distant past? Or, do you believe—really believe—that you were made to have authority over the enemy and all his devices? If you do, are you willing to put on the armor of God and fight?

Let's take a look at the issue of God-given authority and how it impacts our pressing on in our journey to advance God's kingdom. But first allow me to tell you my story of how I discovered the truth that God will fight for us, but we must be willing to trust Him. Every marriage has its high points and low points. I was in a low point when I decided years ago that my husband was consumed by his work (taking care of physical hearts) but that he did not care about my heart (emotional that is). Women I can hear you now saying: "That is my story." Truth be told, women, we have a higher need-to-not-be-ignored scale than our spouses, right? I did not feel valued, loved, affirmed, and you know the rest if you are a woman with a high need-to-not-be-ignored scale. So I decided that he either no longer loved me or I no longer loved him or we no longer fit together. I am laughing as I write this and think of an email I recently saw about a man and woman's diary. Here it is:

Her diary:

"Tonight I thought my husband was acting weird. We had made plans to meet at a nice restaurant for dinner. I was shopping with my friends all day long, so I thought he was upset at the fact that I was a bit late, but he made no comment on it. Conversation wasn't flowing, so I suggested that we go somewhere quiet so we could talk. He agreed, but he did not say much. I asked him what was wrong; He said, ' Nothing.' I asked him if it was my fault that he was upset. He said he wasn't upset, that it had nothing to do with me and not to worry about it. On the way home I told him that I loved him. He smiled slightly. I can't explain his behavior. I don't know why he did not say 'I love you too.' When we got home I felt as if I had lost him completely as if he wanted nothing to do with me anymore. He just sat there quietly and watched TV. He continued to seem distant and absent. Finally with silence all around us I decided to go to bed. About 15 minutes later, he came to bed, but I still felt that he was distracted and his thoughts were somewhere else. He fell asleep— I cried. I don't know what I am to do. I am almost sure that his thoughts are with someone else. My life is a disaster."

His Diary:

"Motorcycle won't start. Can't figure out why."

So you get my point. Women and men simply live on two separate planets. Back to my story. I was in one of those seasons of feeling this way.

I was weary of the marriage battle and determined to fight this God's way. Reading self-help books did not help. Cooking better meals (that was a miracle) didn't help. And every other self-determined way did not work. But God..... began to lead me beside the still waters and restore my soul. He showed me that I was in a battle for my marriage; that my perspective was upside down and that I needed to fight. The good news is He reminded me that the battle belonged to Him. So I slapped on my armor and prepared for the fight ... And the fight was for the renewal of my mind. It is so easy to believe a lie and the lie will continue to grow until we take our authority in Jesus name and ask the Lord to fight for us. Perhaps you need a refresher on Ephesians 6. Here are my cliff notes. Strap on your armor and having done all you can ... STAND. So I asked the Holy Spirit to direct my steps and reposition my heart. The one thing the enemy is determined to do is destroy marriages so beware. You cannot fight this assault alone. You must not lean on your own understanding (Proverbs 3:5) but be determined to take your authority in Christ and use His Word as your sword in the battle. I repositioned my heart by asking the Holy Spirit to show me the truth, and God fought the battle. And to this day this strategy of warfare works whether you are battling for your marriage, your health, or your children. Get God's perspective—seek Him, pray Ephesians 6, and stand. God will fight for you.

The Role of the Redeemed

As God's redeemed—that is, sinners bought and paid for by Jesus—we Christians are to joyfully live and breathe and proclaim the good news to those He brings into our lives. We are also to be joyfully proactive in our response to the assaults on the advancement of the kingdom of God in our personal lives and the world in which we live. The King of the universe has called us to devise and implement strategies to penetrate and weaken the influence of evil. We are God's "Plan A," and there is no "Plan B."

Satan wants to divert people from the love of God. He is bent on the destruction of Christ's kingdom. It sounds crazy, doesn't it? Really, at best, the idea of a war raging between the forces of good and evil sounds made-up, right? I know it does. I know it seems crazy. I am also certain that Satan is counting on that. Satan is counting on this whole war-between-good-and-evil-for-our-souls thing sounding radical—even loony—to all human beings, all the people God loves and wants deep relationship with, people like you and me.

But the good news is that the war has already been won. We can press on knowing that God saw the war coming before time began, and He secured the final victory before you and I breathed our first breaths. He made us to play integral parts in this incredible drama by sharing this great news with anyone and everyone He brings into our lives. But for all who are willing to do that – *be prepared for a battle*. You can bet the enemy will declare war! So what do we do then?

We put on the armor, show up ready for battle, and follow the Captain wherever He leads.

Do you remember your World War II history? On June 6, 1944 -- "D-Day" -- the Allied powers landed on the beaches at Normandy, France, and launched the largest amphibious invasion in the history of the world. The battles over the next several weeks were incredibly dangerous and bloody — Allied casualties alone were estimated at ten thousand — but the invasion was successful. For all intents and purposes, the war in Europe was won as a result of the D-Day invasion, but the fighting continued until May 8, 1945; VE Day was not declared until almost a year after D-Day.

So it is for us Christians and this war in which we find ourselves, this "war to end all wars." Jesus Christ died on the cross over two thousand years ago, and with His last breath on the cross and His resurrection from the grave three days later, He declared D-Day. He conquered death once and for all, and He conquered the enemy: victory was -- and is -- His. But still, we time-bound believers are at war; Christ's followers continue to fight the enemy, who prowls around, seeking whomever he can devour. (See 1 Peter 5:8).

The Great News Continues

Now here is more great news: We have authority over the enemy. It is worth repeating: You and I and anyone who believes Jesus is who He says He is and that He has done all He's said He's done — we who believe God is as good as His Word — we have authority over Satan! We were made to defeat him. Jesus' victory on the cross ensures believers of the power and authority to put the devil in his place. The apostle John stated it this way: "He that is in you is greater than he that is in the world" (1 John 4:4 paraphrased).

Our King and Captain is greater than the enemy who prowls around. We may give Satan a foothold for a little while, but when we come back to our senses, we have the authority to send him flying. John Eldredge makes it even clearer:

> *"The thief comes only to steal and kill and destroy; I have come that they may have life to the full."* (John 10:10)[17]

"Have you ever wondered why Jesus married those two statements? Did you even know he spoke them at the same time? I mean, he says them in one breath. And he had his reasons. By all means, God intends life for you. But right now that life is *opposed*. It doesn't just roll in on a tray. There is a thief. He comes to steal and kill and destroy. In other words, yes, the offer is life, but you're going to have to fight for it because there is an Enemy in your life with a different agenda."

The enemy wants you to be scared, to cower; he wants you to feel powerless; he doesn't want you to learn about the authority you have in Christ. He would like nothing more than to defeat you anytime he wants. And he will do everything he can to keep you from learning the truth about the authority you have over him and exercising that authority.

Using His Authority

Some battles we face are battles of the flesh (the unspiritual person); some are battles caused by the influences of the world; and some are sent from the devil and his cohorts. Let's begin to use the authority God has given us as Christ followers. Let's learn how to take a stand against the enemy's onslaughts, against the spiritual warfare leveled at us as individuals and as the church community, the body of Christ.

For we do not wrestle against flesh and blood, but against the rulers, against the authorities, against the cosmic powers over this present darkness, against the spiritual forces of evil in the heavenly places. (Ephesians 6:12)

Think about the authority a police officer has. If you run a stoplight or rob a store or are in a traffic accident, the officer has the authority to give you a ticket, arrest you, or write up an accident report. We have written laws that grant this authority. The value of this authority rests in the power behind the authority, in this case the elected lawmakers, the government.

In *The Believer's Guide to Spiritual Warfare*, Thomas White quotes Jesus to remind us of the heavy responsibility we have as leaders: "As you sent me into the world, I have sent them into the world." With that in mind, White says, "Spiritual authority is to be exercised to overcome evil on a personal level, and to help set others free from sin and Satan."[18]

We are called to be in the world and not of it, to exercise the authority Jesus clearly has given us, and to confront everyday battles in our lives from our position in Christ.

Seated in Heavenly Places

In his letter to the church in Ephesus, Paul instructed the believers in their walk with Christ and explained how to confront the battles they face. He also gave them this encouraging news: "God raised us up with Christ and seated us with him in the heavenly realms . . . in order that in the coming ages he might show the incomparable riches of his grace expressed in his kindness to us in Jesus Christ" (Eph. 2:6–7). He prayed that the spiritual eyes of the Ephesians would be open to know the hope to which they were called and the power that they had to fulfill their call in Christ (1:18–19). And he reminded them to live a life worthy of their call, walking in holiness and standing against the schemes of the evil one. (4:1, 22–32; 6:13)

In essence, Paul was telling them, and subsequently all believers through the ages, that there are four reasons we are able to effectively confront the battles of life with our position and power in Christ:

1. We are seated with Him in heavenly places.
2. The same Holy Spirit power that raised Jesus from the dead is available to us.
3. Walking in holiness empowers us with authority from Christ.
4. We can proactively stand against the enemy's schemes.

Have you ever meditated on the fact that you are seated in heavenly places? Although you are physically here, as a believer you are spiritually seated with Christ, and He sits at the right hand of the Father. Stop for a moment and think about that. Let it sink in. Isn't it absolutely amazing?

If we can grasp that truth, if we can know it deep down without a doubt, doesn't it have to radically change the way we face the interruptions and trials and struggles life throws in our paths?

When I find myself in the heat of some battle or other, I try to envision myself seated with Christ—the King of kings sitting next to me—having His mind and drawing from His knowledge and wisdom.

Resurrected Power

Let's take a moment to reflect on this truth: we have the same power available to us that raised Christ from the dead:

> I pray that the eyes of your heart may be enlightened in order that you may know the hope to which he has called you, the riches of his glorious inheritance in the saints *and his incomparably great power for us who believe.* That power is the same as the mighty strength he exerted when he raised Christ from the dead and seated him at his right hand in the heavenly realms. (Eph. 1:18–20; emphasis added)

Stop and take this in. The same power that raised Christ from the dead is available to us who believe.

Walking in Holiness: Where the Rubber Meets the Road

How do we make room for God's authority and power? How can we expect to call on that power and authority in our daily lives? Paul made it crystal clear in the fourth chapter of Ephesians. He had just told the new Christians at Ephesus that they have position and power in Christ Jesus, but now comes the hard part. Paul said that the authority we have is *dependent on how we live our lives: "I urge you to live a life worthy of the calling you have received. Be completely humble and gentle, be patient, bearing with one another in love."* (vv. 1–2)

It is one thing to have power and position, and it is quite another to be humble and patient. That's a tall order for some of us, isn't it? Paul doesn't let us off the hook. He told the Ephesians it was time to quit acting like infants tossed back and forth by false teachings and instead grow up and speak the truth in love (vv. 14–15). Now he's done it. He has invaded our personal lives and is pressing on every nerve. We must live lives worthy of the call. In order to bring God's power and authority to bear, we must live out Jesus' humility and gentleness and patience and love. We must extend to others the same grace that the King of kings has extended time and again to us. We must walk in holiness in the here and now, in the midst of our less-than-perfect lives and the war raging all around us. This is where the rubber meets the road.

Walking the Talk

My grown-up, married daughter was going through some trials this week. Sage that I am, I instructed her in the strategies of spiritual battle. I told her to remember her position seated with Christ and her power available through the resurrection, but I saw that it was time to speak the truth in love. It was not easy for me to tell this daughter I love so much that her walk did not match her talk. That is what I felt I must do, though. Truth be known it wasn't easy. I heavily weighed the risk of telling her what I thought, even hurting her versus knowing she needed to hear the truth. I told her that if she wanted authority over the junk going on in her life, she needed to walk in a manner worthy of her calling in

Christ. I did pretty well. My daughter wasn't too pleased. But in the end she took the high road, the highway of holiness. For those of us who do not like confrontations (isn't that everyone?) it can be so difficult. The best way to confront people whether it is your child, friend, or spouse, is to remember God gives grace to the humble and if our motives are good (to help the person) and not selfish, God pours out His grace. The end result is in His hands. The fruit is eternal, and we may never see it. So for me, the litmus test is to have a heart check to see what my motives are before confronting the person. God always meets me on the side of the street where His grace flows when I follow His lead and wait on His timing.

This is where we often detour or crash in our battles. We want the power and the position that Christ gives us, but we do not want to make the sacrifice; we are not so excited about putting off the old self and putting on the character of Jesus. Easier said than done. But that is exactly what we must do in order to claim the King's promises of power and authority.

Ready to Stand

Paul made it clear that after we recognize and accept that we are seated with Christ, we can draw from His power and walk in holiness. Notice that we are *seated*, which means it is *His* effort that wins the battles, not ours. Now, finally, we are ready to stand—but only in His power, not ours: *"Finally, be strong in the Lord and in his mighty power,"* we are told. *"Put on the full armor of God so that you can take your stand against the devil's schemes."* (Eph. 6:11)

Church, it's time to wake up, rise up, and grow up in our recognition that we must never give up, never surrender. In Christ we are able; we are positioned in heavenly places, and the victory is ours.

Battles Close to Home

I may be headed for trouble now. I'm going to get personal. But you know what?

Taking authority in the name of Jesus, with His power, begins *at home*--my home and your home. God's instructions for spreading the good news about Jesus and the kingdom of God begin at home. The Spirit-filled Christ followers were to start in Jerusalem because that is where they were. Then, from Jerusalem they were to go to Judea and Samaria and . . . the ends of the earth. His strategy for exercising kingdom authority was to begin first at home. The parable of the talents illustrates this principle as well: *"You have been faithful with a few things,"* the master told his servants; *"I will put you in charge of many things."* (Matt. 25: 23) What has God put you "in charge of"? Have you been faithful? Faithfulness starts at home. So we start at home and begin with issues related to our here and now, things that personally concern us:

- our children
- our finances
- our relationships
- our jobs

If we cannot take care of our households, how can we use the authority God has given us to influence the world in which we live?

Here's the deal: if the enemy can cause chaos in our families through his assaults, we will become consumed with those things, so stirred up that we will not be able to exercise our authority in our own households, let alone beyond them to impact our world. The enemy has sent out his assignments through things like alcohol and drugs, destruction of relationships, and promiscuity, and if you allow it, Satan will keep you ineffective in Jerusalem -- your home -- and unable to push beyond the barriers there to impact the world around you. Don't try to take on "Judea, Samaria, and the ends of the earth" until you have committed to use your authority at home.

How Do We Take Care of "Jerusalem"?

How do we take care of our "Jerusalem" and exercise the authority Jesus has given us and not allow the enemy to frustrate us and take our focus off our Lord? We must use the tools that God has given us through His Word, the disciplines of the faith.

We must not neglect our own homes in order to serve the world. First caring for our families and households, we can then better serve others. Paul writes Timothy, his protégé, advising him concerning issues that were arising in Ephesus. When Paul left Timothy in Ephesus, he was charged with instructing the church in the way Christians should behave. He knew that one way unbelievers would know Christ was through observing the actions of Christians; therefore, he gives instructions to the church. Chapter five in I Timothy gives specific ways to bring honor to the name of Christ. Primarily Paul is focused on how we must care for widows, and tucked in this chapter is the instruction to provide for our households and the implications of not doing so: *"But if anyone does not provide for his relatives, and especially for members of his household, he has denied the faith and is worse than an unbeliever."* (I Timothy 5:8) Quite a sobering word!

Friends, our Jerusalem is our family, our households that God has entrusted to us. As a woman in ministry, one of my biggest challenges has been that of not neglecting my family. There are so many people and things that compete for my time, and it is easy to fall prey to helping them at the expense of my family. I have a very large family. My husband, aging parents, three children, two sisters, eleven grandchildren, nephews and nieces, the list goes on. Most days it is a battle to remember that God entrusted them into my care and they must be my first priority. Truly they are a gift from God, a treasure to be honored and valued. Jerusalem is where the Gospel, the Good News of Christ was launched. Our families need us to be a carrier of the Good News. If we are reaching the world for Jesus but have not invested in reaching the lost within our own households Paul sees this as a serious offense, equating it with being worse than an unbeliever!

Who Is Our Enemy?

Any good general needs to know who the enemy is before he or she builds an effective battle plan. We know the battle belongs to the Lord, but we must also know how to cooperate with Him for victory. That requires discerning the reasons for our battles, the ploys of the enemy. The book of James illustrates the battle on all fronts: the world, the flesh, and the devil. The battles begin in the flesh with our own stuff, progress into the influence the world has on us, and then move into the demonic. Here are some questions you need to ask to determine the kind of battle you are fighting:

Is the Battle of the World, Flesh or Devil?

Is the battle I'm facing one of the world? Am I approaching this battle with a secular or a biblical worldview? The world teaches us to be independent and self-assured, to look deep within for the answers. Christian teaching is the opposite: Jesus teaches us to be centered on Him, dependent on Him. He very clearly wants us to be God-assured and to look to Him for the answers: *"But seek first the kingdom of God and his righteousness, and all these things will be added to you"* (Matthew 6:33).

If the Battle Is of the Flesh . . .

Can I confront the battle with God confidence, or does the way I live my life get in the way?

As Christians, we are growing to be more like Christ. In the areas of our lives where sin reigns, where we are unforgiving, bitter, dishonest, gossiping, addicted—whatever runs contrary to living in the Spirit—we cannot effectively fight our battles. Those things get in the way. It would be like going to battle with so much baggage that when it's time to move forward and engage in combat we are too weighed down to lift a weapon in defense let alone go on the offensive. Scripture tells us that the wages of sin are death, but in Christ we have eternal life. (Romans 6:23). We also know that not only did He die to bring us life in Him, but He offers us forgiveness *now* when we fail and miss the mark of His highest and best for us. That is the baggage we carry—the result of missing the mark. We go to battle with the burden of sin such as guilt, anger, shame and a myriad of other things and we are left defenseless, without armor. So what are we to do when we are ineffective because of the weight of our sin? We turn to Christ and seek His help. We ask Him to forgive us. We turn our heavy basket over and ask Him to take it, and He does. Now you are battle ready, free to press on.

If the Battle Is of the Devil . . .

Has the battle taken on a life of its own? Can I press through to victory, or am I finding myself unable to press through?

The enemy will ride in on our hurts, places that need healing, our carnality; and he will find a foothold. He is very capable of causing even our best efforts to fail. He will whisper lies in our ears, and if we listen— if we allow him a foothold of any kind—he will delight in pushing us off course. He wants you to get weary in your spiritual journey. But God keeps saying, "Press on; climb higher; don't give up."

A few years ago, my husband and I traveled to Idaho when the hollyhocks were in full bloom. Every one hundred years, the seeds, having been dormant in the ground until just the right time, breakthrough in a magnificent display of God's splendor. We decided to hike up the mountain where we heard the hollyhocks were especially glorious. After hiking halfway, lugging our camera equipment, we saw the hollyhocks and began unpacking the equipment to photograph the scene. But a little old lady with a cane, who was coming down the mountain, saw us. "Don't stop here," she said, pointing uphill. "The best is yet to come."

I wanted to ignore her. My heart was beating out of my chest with exhaustion, and my legs were trembling, but her words echoed in my ears. We began to climb higher. We had come this far . . .

When we finally reached the top, we saw the most spectacular array of flowers I have ever seen. From one end of the mountain to the other at the peak we could see nothing but hollyhocks. Had we stopped halfway, we would have missed the best.

How like our spiritual lives this is as we press on in our journey with Christ. We get weary along the way. We settle for what is good enough when God is calling us higher. It is imperative that we keep pressing on; the best is yet to come.

The following day we chose another hike, to Ants Basin. We climbed and climbed and, once again, exhausted from the climb and the heavy equipment, we stopped to photograph. Would you believe that another old lady came hiking down the mountain, really skipping down? By now I was thinking she must be a messenger from God because her message was the same as the first hiker's: "Don't stop here. The most stunning photo opportunities are ahead."

Who cares? I thought. *I'm tired, thirsty, and ready to get on with it.* But recalling the previous day's discovery, we kept going. We climbed . . . and climbed . . . and climbed until we reached the top.

I was stunned at the marvelous view from the mountaintop, and God spoke to my heart: *Joanne, never give up; never surrender; keep climbing to the best. Don't settle, but instead take this perspective from the mountaintop into the valley of life.*

We are called to keep climbing. It is in the journey that our hearts are resuscitated.

The early American pioneers faced profound struggles in a land that was uncultivated, filled with wild animals, and in need of much work. But they knew that they were called to break new ground and press on to their highest post. We, too, are called to be pioneers—not settlers. Once we settle in our Christian journey, the enemy of our souls lulls us into apathy not wanting us to press on, because he knows the best is yet to come. It is time to wake up and start climbing to the heights.

This is our finest hour as we press on, never surrendering but instead getting a God perspective from the mountaintop that we can release in the valley. This is the spiritual life to which we are called. This is the life where our hearts beat with passion for Christ, knowing that the battles we face are His. He fights for us as we press on.

Remember, even as we're climbing higher and higher in our journey with Christ, we battle from a position of being seated with Christ in heavenly places. Our battles are won from a place of His victory, a place of rest *in* Him. The key to every battle is to remember that we are seated *with* Christ. He has already won *His* battle against the world, the flesh, *and* the devil. As we press into Him, He will help us with our daily battles to overcome things such as addictions, fears, anger, self-condemnation, and the list is endless. Jesus is our hope. He fought for us on the cross, and His victory is ours as we seek Him. Recalling what we said at the beginning of this chapter, our physical hearts need exercise both to keep us healthy and to give us physical energy. Our spiritual hearts also need to be exercised. The way to win the battles that we face every day is to reposition our spiritual hearts in the Word, and to abide in the Vine receiving the power, strength and authority to withstand the assaults.

PART III

Grow Up - Renew

CHAPTER 10

Intentional Change

Do you like change? Some people do—but most don't. Change can be stressful or exhilarating. It can make your heart beat faster out of fear or from excitement. Regardless of how you view change, it is inevitable. Change must take place if we are overweight or we have unhealthy habits. These things threaten the health of our physical hearts, and the cardiologist will tell us that we must make these changes in order to ensure our health. My husband once told me that he tells his heart patients that are extremely overweight that if they don't make lifestyle changes it is as though they are sitting on the train track waiting for the train to run over them. Now I must say that his style is not mine. He is very direct. I cringed when he told me his method of helping these patients. However, he followed up by telling me that he cares enough to tell them that without change they might die. It's serious business taking care of physical hearts, and it is serious business taking care of our spiritual hearts. We must allow the Holy Spirit to renew our hearts and that often involves making changes.

Scripture is full of examples where big changes occurred. God called Abraham to leave his home country, and to go somewhere he had never even been. As if that were not a tall enough order, He also called Abraham to become the father of many nations. Abraham was promised a son, and he would have the promised child-heir when he was old—so old that his wife, Sarai, laughed when she heard about it.

Nevertheless, Abraham was obedient. He left his country, family, and friends and set out to follow God's call. He hadn't asked for that change of plans for his life, but when it came, he followed.

Sometimes change is instigated by God, sometimes it is by our own instigation, and other times it is by chance. But the change I want us to look at together is *intentional change*, the kind of change that occurs when we consider our lives and see a need to do something different. It may be in our workplace, or in our relationships, or maybe we need to make a financial decision. As people who trust God, we examine our lives under the lens and scrutiny of the Holy Spirit, asking, "God, what would You have me do?"

David, the king of Israel, sought the Lord for counsel and invited Him to daily search his soul and give him direction concerning any changes needed in His life. *"Search me, O God, and know my heart!" he wrote. "Try me and know my thoughts!"* (Ps. 139:23 ESV) On this side of the cross, we have the Holy Spirit, the *paraclete*, who leads us into truth, guiding and directing our lives and helping us know what intentional changes we must make to be in line with God's will. He will even prepare you for the road ahead. Jesus promised that the Spirit would *"guide you into all the truth, for he will not speak on his own authority, but whatever he hears he will speak, and he will declare to you the things that are to come."* (John 16:13)

Paul understood the need for intentional change via God's direction. He was a surrendered man who lived for Christ alone. His life's purpose was to intentionally seek Christ *and* make him known. (See 1 Cor. 2:2). His former life of prestige meant nothing. His present life as an apostle meant little more. His life was positioned in a place of having been renewed in mind, allowing God to lead His life. In his letter to the church in Rome, he described the renewed mind's ability to know God's will: "Do not be conformed to this world, but be transformed by the renewal of your mind, that by testing you may discern what is the will of God, what is good and acceptable and perfect" (Rom. 12:2 ESV). Paul's surrendered life in Christ was open to change as the Lord directed. He knew that following Christ meant death to his self-interests and desires and openness to Christ's purposes. (See Phil. 3:8)

Paul expressed that he was a contented man following God's will, and he exemplified intentional life changes to follow Him. (See Phil. 4:11) For example, Paul left a life of power and status to follow Christ. He intentionally left his former life to follow Christ, and in so doing He found true life. His heart began to beat with a new sound, the sounds of heaven, laced with the songs of eternity.

I imagine that his former life was not all it was cracked up to be. In the book of Acts, we see Paul bent on destroying the Christian sect called the Way. (See Acts 9). But on the road to Damascus, Jesus spoke to him, commissioning him to a new life. Paul was confused, blinded for three days by the light of Christ, and my guess is that was plenty of time to think about this God-encounter. I suspect it was in his state of being physically blind that he discovered his need for change.

Ananias was sent to Paul to open his eyes, and the rest is history. Paul never looked back. Step-by-step he evaluated his life, no longer under the law but under grace, making the necessary changes empowered by the Holy Spirit.

What changes do you sense that God is calling you to consider?

Recently I sensed the Lord calling me to move. I wasn't sure it was the Lord, so I prayed and waited before approaching my husband with the news. If it was God's leading, then my husband would have to be all in. I knew he had no desire to move and that my inkling would appear to come out of left field. But the Lord opened the doors needed, and we bought our home. It was an unanticipated change but one I believe the Lord was in. The house is His, and I can't wait to see how we can use it for the kingdom!

As Christians, we are called to a new way of life, a life of flexibility as God leads us into His intended purposes. Earlier we discussed having to let go of something old in order to embrace something new. Change often requires letting go of something. It always involves surrender. The real issue, then, becomes trust. Often our unwillingness to change is directly related to a lack of trusting God.

Recently, reading through the book of Ephesians, I was struck by my need for change in an area of my life where I recognized that I was stuck because I did not wish to let go of control. We all find ourselves at times on the hamster wheel, holding tight to something, yet knowing our need for change and feeling the tension between the two.

King David found himself in this untenable position between the tension of sinning to get whatever he wanted and repenting of his self-indulgent lifestyle. After getting what he wanted at a high cost, he found himself at the mercy of God, needing forgiveness and knowing that change was in order.

One day David noticed Bathsheba, a beautiful woman—but a married woman. She was married to Uriah, a soldier who was at war. David committed adultery with Bathsheba, and she became pregnant. Because Uriah was at war, it would be clear the child was not his own. David's answer was to have Uriah killed on the battlefield. David wanted what he wanted, and he got himself into a pile of trouble. One sin led to another: first adultery, then murder. Ultimately, God took his son.

Intentional change came because David's hand was forced. He knew he could not continue down this path of self-indulgence, and he begged for mercy:

"Have mercy on me, O God, according to your steadfast love; according to your abundant mercy blot out my transgressions.
Wash me thoroughly from my iniquity, and cleanse me from my sin!
For I know my transgressions, and my sin is ever before me.
Against you, you only, have I sinned and done what is evil in your sight,
so that you may be justified in your words and blameless in your judgment.

Behold, I was brought forth in iniquity, and in sin did my mother conceive me.
Behold, you delight in truth in the inward being, and you teach me wisdom in the secret heart.
Purge me with hyssop, and I shall be clean;
wash me, and I shall be whiter than snow." (Ps. 51:1–7 ESV)

Friends, let's face it. Sometimes the change needed in our lives is forced because of our rebellion. Our stubbornness causes us to get into trouble, and then we find ourselves at the mercy of God and in need of change. David wasn't the only one in the Bible who struggled with a need for a change of heart. The impulsive apostle Peter was a free spirit who in many ways needed a dose of humility. He jumped out of a boat to follow Christ on the water, and did a fine job for a moment — then sank. Later, he also impetuously cut off a man's ear! (See John 18:10). He said he would never forsake Christ — never — but he did. And in the end, change was inevitable. As a Christ follower, Peter needed to change. He needed Christ more than he needed to run the show. He did not intentionally change, however. It took a broken heart — broken over his lack of loyalty, his denial of Christ — that finally led him down the road to necessary change.

Following Christ leaves little room for self-rule. It requires that we change, and change requires surrender, and surrender requires trust.

But sometimes we just don't want to change or trust or surrender. God wants us to do these things, but it's not always *convenient* to obey God, is it?

Though we may often find it inconvenient — sometimes *extremely* so — we need to obey God. We have to make it a priority. We have to do things we don't always want to do.

Have you seen those messages from God on various billboards along the highway? They have been all over the internet and in mass distributed e-mails too. I like them because they give the answer to the *Do-I-have-to?* question in a number of ways. For example:

- My way *is* the highway.
- What part of *No* do you not understand?
- We need to talk.
- They are not called The 10 *Suggestions*.
- Keep using my name in vain; I'll make rush hour longer.
- What part of thou shalt didn't you understand?
- You know that *Love Thy Neighbor* thing? I meant it.

All of these messages are signed, *God*. And all of them are telling us the same thing: God is sovereign, and obedience is necessary to fulfill His purposes.

So how do we know if God is requiring something of us? How can we know what He desires and what changes need to be made? Ezekiel found the secret of knowing God and finding His heartbeat. He found that in God's holy presence, his willingness to follow Him would change from a "*have to*" to a "*want to*." There is just something about being in the presence of God that is a heart changer. Do you recall my story about the season in my marriage where I was certain that my husband no longer loved me? By spending time with the Lord, praying, reading Scripture, drawing near to Him, my heart changed. My husband did not change, but hanging out with God changed me; and my change impacted him.

Send Me

The year that King Uzziah died, the prophet Isaiah had a vision of God seated on a throne in the temple (Ezek. 6:1). What an incredible gift this vision was. It was a genuine representation of God's glory and hugeness and holiness. Isaiah saw the seraphs — six-winged celestial beings — and he heard them "calling to one another," praising God: *"Holy, holy, holy is the LORD Almighty; the whole earth is full of his glory."* (v. 3) In this astonishing larger-than-life moment, standing in God's holy presence, Isaiah recognized his own sin and was absolutely undone. *"Woe to me!" he cried. "I am ruined! For I am a man of unclean lips, and I live among a people of unclean lips, and my eyes have seen the King, the LORD Almighty."* (v. 5)

Upon hearing Isaiah's confession, the seraphs took a burning coal from the fire and touched the prophet's lips with it — taking his sin and guilt away — and Isaiah reported, *"Then I heard a voice of the LORD saying, 'Whom shall I send? And who will go for us?' And I said, 'Here am I. Send me!'"* (v. 8) In that profound instant, Isaiah was commissioned, sent out by the King of the universe to fulfill the destiny for which he was created. Once Isaiah saw God's hugeness and holiness and perfect righteousness, he was never the same. His sin glinted and burned in the blazing light of God's sanctity and sovereignty. And once he was cleansed, Isaiah's response could only be: *Send me.*

The Essence of Obedience

If we can just get a glimpse of the holiness of God — of His amazing presence — our desire to serve Him will be ignited. The reverential fear of the Lord — the genuine recognition of God's hugeness and absolute authority — leads to obedience. It has to, doesn't it? It seems to me that gladly following the instruction of the perfect leader without asking *Do I have to?* is the essence of obedience. Think about it: would the perfect leader, the Father who knows best, ever ask you to do something that was unnecessary or superfluous? Would that make any sense?

Oswald Chambers reminds us that God did not address the call to Isaiah; Isaiah was simply in the presence of God and overheard Him asking, "Who will go for us?" So, says Chambers, the call is not for the special few but for everyone.[19]

God called; Isaiah responded. When we are in the presence of God, it is easy to intentionally follow Him when He calls. In God's presence our fear of change and the challenges of obedience fall at His feet. And the best part? Our hearts begin to beat again. We find purpose in His presence.

Just as our physical hearts must be connected to a power source, our spiritual hearts must be connected to a power source. The electrical system of our heart is the power source that makes the atria and ventricles working together contract and relax to pump blood through our hearts. Our spiritual hearts must be connected to the power source of the Presence of God. It is in our connection to Him that our spiritual hearts receive His love and are able in obedience serve Him faithfully in obedience.

At the heart of it all is our free will. But sometimes our will simply says no. Perhaps we have drifted from His presence and His will, or we are stressed, burdened, and busy with life and have made little space for God's still, small voice. And the thought of change . . . well, that is just too much.

When God Says Go and We Say No

You know what happens when we ask God, "Do I have to"? We find reasons not to do what He asks.

But here's the problem: if we disobey God, our spiritual growth is stunted; our spiritual ears become dull, and our ability to hear His voice is inhibited. Why? Because our reasoning crowds out the space for God; our excuses fill our thinking space with reasons that keep us from obeying.

One of my grandsons is so funny. His mother was working with him to teach him that it is not okay to hit the other children in school. The other day on the way to school he said, "Mommy, would it be okay if I hit someone today?" Can you imagine my daughter saying, "Well, all right, honey—but just today." Her little boy had figured out that generally it was not okay to hit the other kids, but then he began to reason that maybe there were some days that it would be okay, sort of like in a card game when there is a wild card that can be anything you want it to be. *Hitting is allowed on Tuesdays and every other Saturday. If Tuesday or Saturday is a national holiday, hitting may occur on the weekday immediately following. When in doubt, ask your mother.*

We are like that sometimes. We hear God speaking and we try to wiggle our way out of it, or at least we search for an opt-out clause, or we reinterpret what we're hearing to match what we would have preferred to hear. Right? We try to find an obedience loophole. The problem is that when we do this, we lose a God-given opportunity to grow in Christlikeness; we give up an opportunity to see God's faithfulness and to experience His nearness.

Fully Persuaded

There are some keys to obeying God's call that we should consider, and Abraham shows us what it takes. Abraham:

- knew His God to be faithful
- was fully persuaded that God could and would do what He said He would do
- knew that God could raise from the dead anything that He took away

The result of Abraham's surrender and obedience is that from this one man came a nation, descendants as numerous as the stars in the sky:

By faith Abraham, when called to go to a place he would later receive as his inheritance, obeyed and went even though he did not know where he was going. . . .

By faith Abraham, when God tested him, offered Isaac as a sacrifice.

He who had received the promises was about to sacrifice his one and only son, even though God had said to him, "It is through Isaac that your offspring will be reckoned." Abraham reasoned that God could raise the dead, and figuratively speaking, he did receive Isaac back from death. (Heb. 11:8, 17–19)

Tucked in the pages of the great faith chapter in the book of Hebrews is one of the essential keys to obeying God. Its writer began by defining faith as the assurance of what we hope for and the certainty of what is unseen. (11:1)

It takes faith not only to obey God, but even to please Him. "Without faith it is impossible to please God," Hebrews 11:6 tells us, "because anyone who comes to him must believe that he exists and that he rewards those who earnestly seek him." And indeed, God pours out His love upon us to motivate us to respond in obedience.

Abraham and the many other biblical men and women of faith were certain of the things that they didn't see because they trusted God. They believed Him for the impossible.

Moving from seeing with our natural eyes to seeing with our eyes of faith requires that we deposit in our "trust account" with God. It is a leap of faith to move from the impossible to the possibilities with God. We do this by getting to know the God of the possibilities. His Word is filled with stories of His faithfulness that fill our "account" and grow our trust.

Are you fully persuaded that God is who He says He is? That *you* are who He says *you* are? Are you fully persuaded that God will do what He says He will do?

These are questions that we all must wrestle with as we seek to grow in our faith. But as we relentlessly, single-mindedly pursue Him, making space for faith in our lives and for His perfect love to fill us and light our way, we will be able to do more than we ever imagined - exceedingly more. He says so. He has said so again and again. And He knows best. Always.

Once we are fully persuaded that His Word is true, when we next hear His call and instruction, we will remember His promises to us. Then, as we each look into the mirror, we will see a mighty warrior there, and we will say with absolute assurance, "Here I am, Lord. Send me."

CHAPTER 11

Born to Love

IF THIS IS to be the finest hour of the church, then we need to recognize that as born-again believers we are born into a lifestyle of love — not natural love, but supernatural, agape love. Agape love is the love we see in the Trinity and the love we see in God's heart toward us. I have been obsessed lately with trying to understand the relationship between the Trinity; the love of the Father, the Son and the Holy Spirit. In my research I came across a theological term known as perichoresis. The word perichoresis comes from two Greek words, *peri* which means around and *chorein* which means to give way or make room. It could be translated as rotation or going around. Perichoresis is not found in the Greek New Testament, but it describes the perfect union of the Trinity and in a sense the dance of the Trinity. This term describes the intimacy, union and harmony between the Godhead. And we are invited into this dance. Yes us! In the beginning, in the Garden, Adam and Eve walked in perfect unity with God, but the fellowship was broken by sin. Jesus sent His Son to restore us back to the place of the Garden; back to the place of harmony. After Jesus was resurrected, the Father sent the Holy Spirit, and we are now invited into the fellowship of Father, Son and Spirit - into the dance of agape love. We are invited into their fellowship to receive love.

As the church is awakened to love, renewal follows. To be renewed means the old is gone and the new is now the *normal*. Peter describes this transformation: *"But you are a chosen race, a royal priesthood, a holy nation, a people for God's own possession, that you may proclaim the excellencies of Him who called you out of darkness into His marvelous light.*" (1 Peter 2:9 ESV)

As God's possession, dearly loved, we have been called out of darkness into the light in order to live in the light of His love. The supernatural love of Christ in us is transforming and uncontainable. It must be poured out on others. And this love that we give to others causes our hearts to beat again. Selfishness or self-love or love with impure motives causes our lives to be flat and unfulfilling. Only God's love satisfies and fills the empty places of our lives.

I once heard it said that the way to truly live a life of contentment is to pour your life out for others — to be others-centered. The problem is we are naturally self-centered, so it is only with God's love having filled our weary souls that we can give to others. The cure for many of the ills of the world is to focus on God and others verses self.

My prayer for my children since they were young was: "Let my ceiling be their floor." I have seen this prayer answered in countless ways, but the most profound way has been in the area of giving. My son over the years has given back on the mission field. When the tsunami hit Sri Lanka, he was in the group of first responders. He did not hesitate to offer help across the world. My two daughters have each exemplified giving too. My older daughter has eight children and a tight budget. Recently she took a little girl shopping whose mother is not involved in her life. My daughter thought it would be good for a little girl being raised by her dad to spend time with another mom. My younger daughter takes in an underprivileged child as much as she is able in order to give this little boy time with a family who can focus on his needs alone. My children have shown me how to give to others. My ceiling of giving is their floor. They have taken my prayer and given it wings. Agape, supernatural God-love, comes from His heart to ours, and in receiving we give it away to others through acts of generosity and caring. Love is Jesus with skin on, and it often involves sacrifice.

As I am writing this, the radio is playing the song "The Things We Do for Love" by 10CC. We all need and want to be loved, and this sometimes drives us to do foolish things. But until we tap into God's love, we know only a love that passes quickly. Paul described God's love versus natural love as a love that will never let us go: "For I am sure that neither death nor life, nor angels nor rulers, nor things present nor things to come, nor powers, nor height nor depth, nor anything else in all creation, will be able to separate us from the love of God in Christ Jesus our Lord" (Rom. 8:38–39 ESV). I have a dear friend who walked through a terrible dark season. Her husband had been having an affair, and her heart was broken. She would call and we would pray on the phone every day for God to work in his heart and for their marriage to be restored. There were friends who told her to leave. How could she stay? Could trust ever be restored? She determined to walk this out God's way, offering him forgiveness, honoring the covenant of marriage, and seeking counsel. My friend had to make a choice to tell her heart to beat again — to believe that God could restore and renew their marriage. She stood her ground that they were one and that God could do the impossible. There were times when my heart broke for her, but she continued to believe, pray, and honor the Lord. She persisted and to this day, her marriage reflects the God of possibilities—the God who steps in when we believe and trust. I know some of you reading this may have been through divorce. Things did not work out for you the same way. But the same God of possibilities offers you renewal. He is the same God that tells your heart to beat again.

Friends, we need to let that soak in. There is nothing that can separate us from God's love, and to me that is the most comforting scripture ever! His love and His forgiveness extended to us enables us to love and extend supernatural agape love to others. And through it all we must know that people may stop loving us. They may turn against us, grow fickle, and turn their backs. But God . . .

He will never forsake us.

The church is in need of renewal, and it is love that is at the center of true renewal. The most poignant picture of love in my opinion is that of Christ and His church, which Paul equated to a marriage union between a man and a woman:

> *Wives, submit to your own husbands, as to the Lord. For the husband is the head of the wife even as Christ is the head of the church, his body, and is himself its Savior. Now as the church submits to Christ, so also wives should submit in everything to their husbands.*
>
> *Husbands, love your wives, as Christ loved the church and gave himself up for her, that he might sanctify her, having cleansed her by the washing of water with the word, so that he might present the church to himself in splendor, without spot or wrinkle or any such thing, that she might be holy and without blemish. In the same way husbands should love their wives as their own bodies. He who loves his wife loves himself. For no one ever hated his own flesh, but nourishes and cherishes it, just as Christ does the church, because we are members of his body. "Therefore a man shall leave his father and mother and hold fast to his wife, and the two shall become one flesh." This mystery is profound, and I am saying that it refers to Christ and the church. However, let each one of you love his wife as himself, and let the wife see that she respects her husband.* (Eph. 5:22–32 ESV)

A church on fire for God, renewed in His love, will transform the world. Love:

- is unconquerable
- is unquenchable
- covers a multitude of sins
- always trusts
- lays down self-life for others

In the words of Paul:

Love is patient and kind; love does not envy or boast; it is not arrogant or rude. It does not insist on its own way; it is not irritable or resentful; it does not rejoice at wrongdoing, but rejoices with the truth. Love bears all things, believes all things, hopes all things, endures all things.

Love never ends. As for prophecies, they will pass away; as for tongues, they will cease; as for knowledge, it will pass away. For we know in part and we prophesy in part, but when the perfect comes, the partial will pass away. When I was a child, I spoke like a child, I thought like a child, I reasoned like a child. When I became a man, I gave up childish ways. For now we see in a mirror dimly, but then face to face. Now I know in part; then I shall know fully, even as I have been fully known. So now faith, hope, and love abide, these three; but the greatest of these is love. (1 Cor. 13:4–13 ESV)

In our self-absorbed society this kind of love seems impossible; it is impossible apart from the love of Christ. Paul was walking the self-absorbed road to Damascus, seeking to persecute the lovers of Christ, but he found himself struck by Christ's love Himself. His self-life was destroyed and his new life became an offering poured out for others as he served Christ.

When I consider people who have loved as Christ loves, Mother Teresa is at the top of my list. Purported to be on her wall in her home was the prayer of Calcutta:

> *People are often unreasonable, illogical, and self-centered.*
> *Forgive them anyway.*
> *If you are kind,*
> *people may accuse you of selfish ulterior motives.*
> *Be kind anyway.*
> *If you are successful,*

you will win some false friends and some true enemies.
Succeed anyway.
If you are honest and frank, people may cheat you.
Be honest and frank anyway. What you spend years
building, someone could destroy overnight.
Build anyway.
If you find serenity and happiness, they may be jealous.
Be happy anyway.
The good you do today, people will often forget tomorrow.
Do good anyway.
Give the world the best you have, and it may never be enough.
Give the best you've got anyway.

Love simply does not depend on how we feel or how we are treated. A renewed church, fully alive, loves as Christ loves, and that is only possible through receiving His love toward us. This can only be understood through the message of the cross—that while we were yet sinners, a total wreck, Jesus died for us, laying down all His rights as God and offering up His life as a sacrifice for us so that we might spend eternity with Him. Preposterous? Yes! Radical? Yes! But as John 3:16 reminds us, God so loved the world that He gave His only Son . . . for us.

I think we have become so accustomed to hearing this scripture that the full impact of what Christ did for us has been lost. Our ears are filled with other thoughts, and our preoccupation with living this life on *earth* has caused us to forget that we were made for *another world*. As the church awakens to the message of Christ's love and experiences an encounter with His radical love, the state of the church will be renewed. Our families will be transformed and renewed as we receive and give Christ's love.

The depths of Christ's love is exhibited on the cross. If you were the only person on the earth, He would have died for you. It was love that led

Him to the cross, love that endured the suffering, and love that held Him on the cross. It was love that uttered, "It is finished." It was love that gave us His promises never to forsake us, to send us His Holy Spirit to come alongside us, to lead and guide us. His Word is filled with His promises born of love.

I saw a sign the other day that I really liked:

What part of *It is finished* do you not understand?

Whoever made that sign was asking us what part of Jesus' finished work on the cross do we not believe. Our Lord's last words were, "It is finished," and He meant it. What His heavenly Father had sent Him into the world to do had been accomplished. Completely and for all time. But at the crossroads of unbelief, we fail to grasp the entirety of what Jesus did for us.

Notice that our crisis of faith lies at the *cross*roads:†: that is where we either throw caution to the wind, take God's Word for it, and allow the Holy Spirit to lead us forward—or we choose not to believe.

Unless the Lord Builds the House

In my quiet time the other morning I came across the scripture *"Unless the LORD builds the house, its builders labor in vain. Unless the LORD watches over the city the watchmen stand guard in vain."* (Ps. 127:1) You know how sometimes a scripture jumps off the page and grabs you and wrestles you to the ground? That's what happened to me with the first two lines of Psalm 127. I sat with those words for what seemed an eternity until I heard God's still, small voice say, *Joanne, if you will allow Me to build, you will be assured of success.*

What was I building without Him? Where and when had I mixed the bucket of cement on my own and started constructing something apart from God?

I recognized that I was depending on my I-can-do attitude rather than doing all things in God's It-is-finished strength. When I read Psalm 127:1, it penetrated my heart and mind, and I was found out; I heard God's Spirit and realized that I could no longer continue building on my own. He had searched my heart and convicted me, and I could not go on building without Him. Why would I want to? I was tired, and the building I was working on had a crack in it.

How about you? What house are you building, what project are you managing, apart from the promises and assurances of God? Your physical house, your spiritual house, your marriage, your job?

God Keeps His Promises

Years ago I was in my daughter's room, making her bed after she had gone to school.

As I was apt to do on occasion, I knelt down by her bed and prayed for her. She was going through a difficult stage, and I needed to consult with God about it. I sensed Him telling me that it was going to be tough to raise her, but that one day she would be a powerful woman of God. Now, she was only eight at the time, and I admit to you that this word was not something I really wanted to hear. Imagine the thoughts and questions I had at that moment. I didn't want to know that I would be facing years and years — how many, O Lord? — of difficult child rearing. Would you?

But God was true to His word. Raising my daughter was like what I imagine riding a bucking bronco would be like. I fell off more than I stayed on. And when the hard times hit, you can be sure that I clung to the promise God made to me that day in her room. And today she is an extraordinary woman. With eight children to raise and a business to run, she does it all —by the grace of God.

How To Walk in God's Promises

To walk in God's promises we must do two things:

1. *Know* His promises by knowing His Word
2. Be filled with the Holy Spirit

Paul made it clear that without the Spirit, God's Word is like a foreign language to us: *"The man without the Spirit does not accept the things that come from the Spirit of God, for they are foolishness to him and he cannot understand them because they are spiritually discerned."* (1 Cor. 2:14) It is the Holy Spirit who enables us to understand and appropriate His Word for ourselves. He helps us to spiritually discern — to see and know — God's promises in His Word, and shows us how to grab hold of them and apply them to our lives, here and now. So how does one go about being filled with the Spirit? Well how do you become filled with anything? You take it in. You drink it. You eat it. As a believer the Holy Spirit comes to dwell in your earthly temple.

Paul informs us that we are the temple of the Holy Spirit and the life of Christ, through His Holy Spirit, makes His home in the hearts of believers. Think about this for a minute. Let it sink in. The Lord of all creation, the Lord of life itself takes up residence in the hearts of those who receive and love Him. Daily we walk, carrying the Presence of Christ, and He leads us by the power of His Spirit within. He leads us into truth and helps us believe His promises and live into His promises. Apart from His Spirit at work in us, His promises would fall on deaf spiritual ears.

Beloved friends, we need the infilling of His Spirit. I liken it to a heart transplant. Ezekiel did too. He told us that one day we would be rid of our heart of stone, and it would be replaced with a new spirit: *"And I will give you a new heart and I will put a new spirit in you."* (Ezekiel 36:26) A physical heart transplant involves getting a donor heart, and that can be difficult.

Jesus Christ was the donor for our spiritual hearts. He laid down His life so that we could have eternal life. A physical heart transplant is done by cutting through the breastbone. Blood flows through a heart-lung bypass machine while the surgeon works on the heart. This machine does the work of the heart and lungs while they are stopped and supplies your body with blood and oxygen. Your diseased heart is removed, and the donor heart is stitched in place. The heart-lung machine is then disconnected. Blood flows through the transplanted heart taking over the work of supplying your body with blood and oxygen.[20] Beloved friends, Jesus Christ performs a heart transplant when we turn from sin and receive Him. He renews our broken spiritual heart and replaces it with His heart breathing the fresh oxygen of His Holy Spirit into our lives.

CHAPTER 12

Putting on the New Man

THE CHURCH IS not just an institution made up of people who are Christians. The church is a body that, when fully functioning, is a game changer — a world changer. Together, a group of laid-down lovers of Jesus Christ, committed to advancing His kingdom and not their own, can change the world in ways we can hardly imagine. The God of possibilities working through men and women who are God-seekers will bring a freshness and newness to a tired world. People are tired of stress, of being overwhelmed with life's circumstances and the changes in our world that induce more stress. Paul described the church as a well-functioning body wherein each part has a significant purpose. Together, this magnificent body, renewed in Christ's image, creates a new normal in a stressed-out world:

> And he gave the apostles, the prophets, the evangelists, the shepherds and teachers, to equip the saints for the work of ministry, for building up the body of Christ, until we all attain to the unity of the faith and of the knowledge of the Son of God, to mature manhood, to the measure of the stature of the fullness of Christ, so that we may no longer be children, tossed to and fro by the waves and carried about by every wind of doctrine, by human cunning, by craftiness in deceitful schemes. Rather, speaking the truth in love, we are to grow up in every way into him who is the head, into Christ, from whom the whole body, joined and held together by every joint with which it is equipped, when each part is working properly, makes the body grow so that it builds itself up in love. (Eph. 4:11–16 ESV)

A healthy heart is able to pump blood throughout the body enabling the body to work as God designed. Similarly, the church body must be filled with the Holy Spirit in order to function as God designed.

Did you notice the key point tucked into the passage in Ephesians ? We are to grow up with Christ as the head and every member of the body functioning together in love.

I hear so much grumbling from the body of Christ that we are losing the war and that Christianity, having been marginalized, is losing its relevancy in a world that is moving in the other direction at warp speed. It is easy to get caught up in the argument that Christianity is losing ground. Of course the history of the church has seen a series of battles lost. But the war was won on the cross. Battles ensue, the world continues to change, but the war fought on the cross is over. Yet, if the enemy can keep our eyes on our losses, we will forget the centrality of the cross — the message that Paul described in Colossians 2:9–15:

> *For in him the whole fullness of deity dwells bodily, and you have been filled in him, who is the head of all rule and authority. In him also you were circumcised with a circumcision made without hands, by putting off the body of the flesh, by the circumcision of Christ, having been buried with him in baptism, in which you were also raised with him through faith in the powerful working of God, who raised him from the dead. And you, who were dead in your trespasses and the uncircumcision of your flesh, God made alive together with him, having forgiven us all our trespasses, by canceling the record of debt that stood against us with its legal demands. This he set aside, nailing it to the cross. He disarmed the rulers and authorities and put them to open shame, by triumphing over them in him. (ESV)*

The profound message that the war has already been won has been forgotten because the daily battles we face have caused us to lose heart. The church is the hope of the world. Yet, we forget that we have been raised to new life. We are not powerless but *powerful*, and together, as the body of Christ, we can bring renewed hope to a world that seems to be spinning out of control.

How do we do this? By putting on the "new man." (See Eph. 4:22–25; Col. 3:8–11). If Jesus died on the cross to offer us a new way of living — we must choose *His way*. As Paul wrote, we must "grow up" with Christ as the head.

I grew up with a silver spoon in my mouth. I remember staying up all night one night crying for a horse, and by morning my dad had told my mother to go and buy me one. I knew I could wear them down. This same attitude marched right into adulthood and reared its ugly head early on in my marriage. I was very demanding.

One day, while I was on the beach with my children, a piece of paper floated right onto our beach blanket. I opened it to find these words:

> *Likewise, wives, be subject to your own husbands, so that even if some do not obey the word, they may be won without a word by the conduct of their wives, when they see your respectful and pure conduct. Do not let your adorning be external—the braiding of hair and the putting on of gold jewelry, or the clothing you wear—but let your adorning be the hidden person of the heart with the imperishable beauty of a gentle and quiet spirit, which in God's sight is very precious. For this is how the holy women who hoped in God used to adorn themselves, by submitting to their own husbands, as Sarah obeyed Abraham, calling him lord. And you are her children, if you do good and do not fear anything that is frightening.*
>
> *Likewise, husbands, live with your wives in an understanding way, showing honor to the woman as the weaker vessel, since they are heirs with you of the grace of life, so that your prayers may not be hindered.* (1 Peter 3:1–7 ESV)

I looked up to heaven and said, "God, did You send this directly to me, special delivery?" I knew that it was a message from Him. As a young Christian woman I desired to live a Godly life, and the message of submission rocked my self-centered world.

I searched this scripture to understand the meaning and discovered it did not mean I was supposed to be a doormat. It simply meant that I was to understand that having two heads in one home was not God's intention. I began to understand that my husband's role, according to the Word, was to lay his life down for me, and my role was to respect him. It was a mutual submission of love and respect. It was time that I understood that Christ wanted me wholly surrendered to Him and from that place of surrender, I could fully love my husband.

This begs the question, how can we live a life of surrendering to Christ? Up to that point I thought I was the center of the universe. But God got ahold of my thinking, transforming my mind with the power of His Word.

So let's get practical. No one wants to surrender and give up control. And few of us wish to die to self. But the truth is, we need to die to the false self—the one that thinks it's all about us. The false self is never content, never at peace. The true self, the one made in God's image, is meant to revolve around our Creator. This self is content and at peace and willing to pour out for others. The true self considers others' interests above their own. Philippians 2 tells us:

> So if there is any encouragement in Christ, any comfort from love, any participation in the Spirit, any affection and sympathy, complete my joy by being of the same mind, having the same love, being in full accord and of one mind. Do nothing from selfish ambition or conceit, but in humility count others more significant than yourselves.
>
> Let each of you look not only to his own interests, but also to the interests of others. Have this mind among yourselves, which is yours in Christ

Jesus, who, though he was in the form of God, did not count equality with God a thing to be grasped, but emptied himself, by taking the form of a servant, being born in the likeness of men.

And being found in human form, he humbled himself by becoming obedient to the point of death, even death on a cross. (vv. 1–8 ESV)

Paul was not able to live a selfless life apart from Christ, and it was not head knowledge that changed him; it was the transforming power of Christ in him that changed him.

Friends, we simply cannot will ourselves to live as Christ lived. We cannot wake up in the morning determined to live selflessly. We simply cannot do it apart from the power of God at work in us. We must clothe ourselves in the Word so that its power will not only shape our thinking but will transform us. We must fill our hearts with His Spirit. Our hearts need to be revived and our lives made new.

Recently, my precious granddaughter came over to spend the night. She asked if she could sleep in the guest room, announcing that she was now a big girl (she's ten). I told her it would be fine for her to stay in the guest room if she did not watch TV.

The children's room does not have a TV, so I knew that was why she wanted to stay in the guest room. Imagine my surprise when she admitted, "Yiayia [that means "grandmother" in Greek], I am not sure that I can keep from watching TV in that room. You know I can be sneaky."

I wanted to laugh out loud but instead said, "Hopie, you are not sneaky. You are trustworthy. That is how God knows you. I trust you."

The next morning, I could hardly wait to see what had transpired. Soon she bounced down the stairs, saying, "Yiayia I was sort of trustworthy. I turned the TV on for a few minutes, but then I realized that I was trustworthy and not sneaky and turned it off." A win for God's team! Though she started to give into the flesh, she turned and chose to put on the new nature of a trustworthy child.

Beautiful women of God, we are not who we think we *are*. We are who God says we are. We are renewed in Christ and we must choose to take off the old self and put on the new self. Paul understood this:

> *Put to death therefore what is earthly in you: sexual immorality, impurity, passion, evil desire, and covetousness, which is idolatry. On account of these the wrath of God is coming. In these you too once walked, when you were living in them. But now you must put them all away: anger, wrath, malice, slander, and obscene talk from your mouth. Do not lie to one another, seeing that you have put off the old self with its practices and have put on the new self, which is being renewed in knowledge after the image of its creator. Here there is not Greek and Jew, circumcised and uncircumcised, barbarian, Scythian, slave, free; but Christ is all, and in all.*
>
> *Put on then, as God's chosen ones, holy and beloved, compassionate hearts, kindness, humility, meekness, and patience, bearing with one another and, if one has a complaint against another, forgiving each other; as the Lord has forgiven you, so you also must forgive.*
>
> *And above all these put on love, which binds everything together in perfect harmony. And let the peace of Christ rule in your hearts, to which indeed you were called in one body. And be thankful. Let the word of Christ dwell in you richly, teaching and admonishing one another in all wisdom, singing psalms and hymns and spiritual songs, with thankfulness in your hearts to God. And whatever you do, in word or deed, do everything in the name of the Lord Jesus, giving thanks to God the Father through him.* (Col. 3:5–17 ESV)

Let's take a look at some of the pearls hidden in this passage as we continue to think about growing up as a body of Christ — working together to impact our world. This passage is cause for our hearts to beat again with the sounds of heaven as we grab hold of the promise that if we will make a choice to get rid of the old and embrace the new, we will find our lives filled with thankfulness. And a grateful heart is medicine for the soul.

So some of the ingredients of our grown-up lives in Christ are compassion, kindness, humility, meekness, and patience. To clothe ourselves in these, we must first rid ourselves of covetousness, idolatry, impatience — not something we can do apart from Christ. The only choice we have is to ask God to change us from the inside out. The only hope we have is to throw ourselves at the feet of Christ and ask Him to change us. It is a work of grace and not one of striving. No pull-yourself-up-by the bootstraps thinking can make a difference. Only the power of God working in each of us can transform. This is the message of the cross. The battle for our hearts was won on the cross, so the new man must be released by God's power.

Now, let's get real. It's easy to love the lovable. But what do we do about the *un*lovable? Is it possible to grow up in Christ and to be renewed in such a way that we deal equally with the lovable *and* the unlovable?

Are there people in your life who drive you crazy? I guess it really depends on what *makes* you crazy, doesn't it? Some people ask you the same rhetorical question over and over again, as if there might be some point to the question (or some answer that would satisfy them). Other people talk for the sole purpose of hearing their own voices and opinions. Still others are just flat-out rude or insensitive or oblivious to the feelings and experiences of those around them. Fill in the blank. You know who they are, and you know what makes you crazy.

People who drive us crazy are, frankly, a fact of life.

And every now and then — like it or not — they are divine appointments, chosen for us by God, as surely as were our parents and sisters and brothers.

So, okay — the question is not, do we have people in our lives who require extra grace? The question is, when those people appear and the making-crazy begins, what do we do about it? What do we do about them?

Making Space, Extending Grace

At the heart of this book is the imperative of making space for the living God in our everyday, 24/7 lives, allowing His Holy Spirit to lead us and teach us how to be like our Lord Jesus, how to follow after Him, how to wake up, rise up, and grow up in Christ. When we are able to deal with these wrong-hearted thoughts of ours, the judgments and attitudes, we make room for love, mercy, and justice. Making space for God involves moving out the things in our lives that run contrary to Him and His heart's desire for us, and moving in the Godly counterparts. As we depose ourselves from the throne of our lives — as each of us takes *me* out of the center and puts Jesus there — our King will have the room required to live and move and have His being *in us*.

You know how I do this? Like repentance, it is an everyday thing, an everyday commitment. Every morning I begin my day by saying, "Self, get off the throne; Lord God, please take Your rightful place on the throne of my life." I know it may sound overly simple, even foolish, but it works for me.

Room for Whom?

Is there room for God in your life, or are your spiritual spaces cluttered with people who are so difficult they end up sucking the life out of you? At the end of the day, do you often find yourself angry, frustrated, *crazy*? You haven't accomplished what you intended to accomplish — all you've done is react to the crazy-makers. Do you end up bitter and resentful toward the people you have invited into those spiritual spaces inside you, the people to whom you have given the most time and energy and attention?

This is not the way relationships are supposed to be, is it? How do we end up there? Maybe you don't, but if I am going to be honest, I must admit that I sometimes find myself drained by a needy person rather than figuring out how to deal with him in a loving and truthful way—in a way that honors him, me, and God.

Remember: God may have brought these people directly to us; if not, He has at least allowed them to be in our lives. Though we are often unable to discern His purposes in the moment, we can be absolutely certain our King never does or allows anything without a perfect purpose.

The Enemy's Trap

In the book of Colossians, we are instructed to clothe ourselves with compassion, humility, gentleness, and patience. (Col. 3:12) But sometimes we aren't able to take off the spirit-smothering apparel of anger, stress, impatience, or judgment; sometimes just the thought of doing so seems draining — let alone putting on the spiritual apparel of love, mercy and justice. This is a trap. And it is just where the enemy wants us: on the hamster wheel dealing with each exhausting encounter. With each encounter we become less and less willing to forge through to God's intent for us, which is to be in deep relationship with Him and to be more like His Son.

So how do we address our reactionary, Spirit-less hamster mentality? How do we climb out of the enemy's trap when dealing with people who are so needy that they drain us?

EGR People

One of my favorite books is *Balcony People* by Joyce Landorf Heatherley. It is about "the lethal poison of rejection and the healing antidote of affirmation."[21] Heatherley distinguishes between worldly affirmation (people pleasing) and Godly affirmation (God pleasing). Extra-Grace-Required people, whom we'll refer to as EGR people, need an extra measure of love and affirmation. They are often wounded, broken, disillusioned, deeply dissatisfied people who wind up being rejected because of their (wounded, broken, disillusioned, deeply dissatisfying) behavior.[22]

Do you know anyone like that? You can see it in them, and if you pay any attention at all, you can see them setting themselves up again and again to fail in relationships. Their brokenness leads the way and their deeply dissatisfying relationships flow out of their hurts, hang-ups, and habits.

More times than I can count, I have wanted to say to these EGR people, "Look at what you're doing! You are driving people crazy — talking incessantly, trying to get attention, always engaging in obnoxious behavior that pushes people away."

The thing is, the EGRs' brokenness and repeated life-draining behavior, and our inability to deal with their needs in ways that will actually honor and change them, keep us on the hamster wheel. This is just where the enemy of abundant life and grace and justice wants us. As long as we're "spinning our wheel," we'll never be able to put on the spiritual apparel of mercy, love, and truthfulness.

What People Need

Here is the truth. People need love and affirmation and grace. I mean *all* people — EGR people, of course, and you and me too. And the same exact love and affirmation and grace (unmerited favor) that God extends to you and me is what we have to extend to the EGR people in our lives.

But how do we get to the place where, not only do we *not* reject EGR people, but we actually begin to bless, affirm, and speak truth-with-love to them?

As the old saying goes, "You cannot give what you don't have." Before we can become affirmers, truth tellers, and mercy givers, we must accept God's mercy ourselves. Yes, we have to be merciful to *ourselves* and deal with our own stuff — the stuff that keeps us on our own hamster wheel — the very things that make us crazy when another EGR person does them or says them.

Jesus made it very clear that we are to love our neighbors as ourselves. (See Matt. 22:39; Mark 12:31). We cannot love others as Christ loves us until we love ourselves as Christ loves us.

So, in addition to the love, affirmation, and grace that we need, we also need mercy — not only from God, but from ourselves. Let me give you an example of how all of this works together.

Oxygen and Grace

We all know the drill when a commercial airplane takes off: the flight attendant goes through the motions of explaining safety measures to all the passengers. Toward the end of her presentation, she tells us that in case of emergency — that is, if the cabin loses pressure — the oxygen masks will drop from overhead (a fitting metaphor); she then holds up an oxygen mask and reminds us that adults traveling with children should put their masks on first before assisting their kids.

The same principle applies to us and the provision of love, truth, affirmation and grace. We must first accept and "put on" God's love for us, loving ourselves the way He loves us, and allow Him to heal our broken wings before we can fly — certainly before we can help others fly. And before we can give the oxygen of extra grace to the unlovable, grace-starved people in our lives, we must first accept it ourselves from the Source of grace.

We cannot extend to others what we do not have ourselves. Doesn't this make perfect sense?

God's Way: Grace Extended

When my granddaughter, Mary Catherine, was twelve years-old, she told me that there was someone at her school who continually lied to her friends. When it happened once again, it was the last straw as far as Mary Catherine was concerned. The girl was spreading lies about Mary Catherine, and my granddaughter's other friends turned on the girl who lied. They decided they did not want to be her friend anymore. They shunned her.

But not Mary Catherine. My granddaughter decided to extend grace. She confronted the girl who had lied about her and asked her what was going on in her life. Mary Catherine did not excuse the girl's behavior but tried to find out what was behind the lying.

The girl told Mary Catherine that her parents were in the middle of a bitter divorce.

She was sad and angry, and she had lied about Mary Catherine because of the way she was feeling.

Mary Catherine listened and understood and offered to help the girl. They agreed that if she would quit lying, Mary Catherine would help her walk through this hard time.

Talk about making a grandmother proud. I wanted to tell everyone the story — even random people I saw that week.

Now, thinking about how my granddaughter extended grace, I wonder if I would have done the same. Or would I have taken the much easier path and joined the other girls and turned my back on the girl who lied? Would I have allowed my initial indignation and hurt and self-righteousness to rule me, withholding the grace that the sad and frightened girl so desperately needed? As Christ followers, we must shed our attitudes of judgment and take on an attitude of grace. And do you know what I have found to be true? When I clothe myself in humility and grace, my heart beats with a new song — a song of mercy and love and selflessness. We must surrender and allow God to strip us of our old habits and responses and take on the ways of Christ. It is a work of the Spirit. We can't do it on our own, but as we stay close to Jesus, we become more like Him.

Putting on the New Life

We all need to take off the spiritless apparel that causes us to be bitter, angry, and frustrated with the people in our lives. God calls us to put on the spiritual apparel of patience, kindness, and mercy, which He designed for us to wear. Paul wrote, *"You were taught, with regard to your former way of life, to put off your old self, which is being corrupted by its evil desires; to be made new in the attitude of your minds; and to put on the new self, created to be like God in true righteousness and holiness."* (Eph. 4:22–24)

Going back to previous chapters, we have positioned ourselves to de-clutter our lives making more space for God. We have looked at letting go of old patterns and embracing new — letting go of the things that we have on life support in order to walk in newness of life with the Holy Spirit leading. We have seen the value in pressing on and never giving up, and of using our gifts for the glory of God. We have learned the importance of putting off the old self and clothing ourselves with Christ. Friends, this is a work of the Spirit. At some point or another, each of us as believers has strived to get this thing right. We have each had seasons of trying to change. If any of you can relate, this message is for you and for me and for every potential world changer: The game changer in the equation is *God*.

CHAPTER 13

No Longer Tossed Around

"I am not ashamed of the gospel," the apostle Paul wrote eloquently, *"for it is the power of God for salvation to everyone who believes, to the Jew first and also to the Greek."* (Rom. 1:16 ESV) Our hearts have been transformed and our lives de-cluttered. Now Church, it is time to tell our hearts to beat again with the power of the gospel — the good news that Christ came, was crucified, rose from the dead on the third day, and is seated today at the right hand of the Father. And as believers, we are seated with Him in heavenly places. Although we are physically positioned on earth, we are spiritually positioned with Christ. Ephesians 2 tells us:

You were dead in the trespasses and sins in which you once walked, following the course of this world, following the prince of the power of the air, the spirit that is now at work in the sons of disobedience—among whom we all once lived in the passions of our flesh, carrying out the desires of the body and the mind, and were by nature children of wrath, like the rest of mankind. But God, being rich in mercy, because of the great love with which he loved us, even when we were dead in our trespasses, made us alive together with Christ—by grace you have been saved—and raised us up with him and seated us with him in the heavenly places in Christ Jesus, so that in the coming ages he might show the immeasurable riches of his grace in kindness toward us in Christ Jesus. For by grace you have been saved through faith. And this is not your own doing; it is the gift of God, not a result of works, so that no one may boast. For we are his workmanship, created in Christ

Jesus for good works, which God prepared beforehand, that we should walk
in them. (vv. 1–9 ESV)

Now think about this with me for a moment. As Christians, we are seated
with Christ. So close that we can hear the sounds of heaven—so close
that when He speaks we hear Him. And as if that isn't enough for your
heart to beat again, think about the fact that Jesus sent His Holy Spirit
to lead, guide, and direct our lives, and He works powerfully within us.

So what is the problem with the church today?

The problem is that the noise of the world has crowded Him out.
What noise? The noise of unbelief, of busyness, and the countless other
philosophies that threaten to dilute the message of Christ. We are overwhelmed with choices and weighted down with life — and we have
lost hope. The enemy . . . He doesn't play fair, and he'll do anything
to minimize the message of the cross and the hope we have in Christ.
Without the cross — without the resurrection — there is no hope for
our future.

For two thousand years Satan has tried to squelch the truth of the
cross, but the followers of the truth persisted. So he looked for other
ways to tear down our hope, like overwhelming us and serving up dead
philosophies to take us down a hopeless path.

The Screwtape Letters, by C. S. Lewis, is a collection of fictional cor-
respondence from a demon named Screwtape to his mentor and nephew,
Wormwood, advising him on how to draw a new Christian away from his
faith. In one interchange we see that the church itself can be helpful in
this endeavor:

The two churches nearest to him, I have looked up in the office. Both have
certain claims. At the first of these the vicar is a man who has been so long
engaged in watering down the faith to make it easier for a supposedly in-
credulous and hard-headed congregation that it is now he who shocks his

parishioners with his unbelief, not vice versa. He has undermined many a soul's Christianity.[23]

There are churches today that have watered down the message of the cross. In order to be more "tolerant," their preachers present the truth of God's Word in a diluted manner so as not to offend. Listen to what Paul had to say about this: "For the word of the cross is folly to those who are perishing, but to us who are being saved it is the power of God. For it is written *'I will destroy the wisdom of the wise, and the discernment of the discerning I will thwart.' Where is the one who is wise? Where is the scribe? Where is the debater of this age? Has not God made foolish the wisdom of the world?.*" (1 Cor. 1:18–20 ESV)

Did you catch Paul's words? "For the word of the cross is folly to those who are perishing, but to us who are being saved it is the power of God." The message of the cross seems like foolishness to some. Paul continued in his defense of the gospel by warning against the philosophers of this age: *"See to it that no one takes you captive by philosophy and empty deceit, according to human tradition, according to the elemental spirits of the world, and not according to Christ."* (Col. 2:8 ESV)

The false teaching among the Colossians was marked by an emphasis on philosophy, but most of all, it was a religion based on "the tradition of men. It had the stamp of *man* on it, not of *God*.

Nineteenth-century scholar Arthur Peake, in his commentary on Colossians, described being taken captive by empty philosophies as being cheated or led away as prey.[24]   It also has the idea of robbing and plundering. The Colossian church was being led away from the message of the cross, and the means of lure were empty philosophies, a mix of early Gnosticism, Greek philosophy, Jewish mysticism, and local mystery religions. What I find interesting is that the philosophy threatening the Colossian Christians was dangerous not because it was overt sinful behavior but because it appealed to the intellect.

Paul was appealing to the Colossian church to accept the message of the power of the gospel to save. His zeal and his deep love for the church were rooted in his understanding of Christ's love for him. Christ had met Paul on the road to Damascus and led him to abandon his old life, and receive new life in Christ. Paul gave up everything to follow Christ, and, in turn, he found everything. He knew that all other philosophies, based on human wisdom and reasoning, would not lead to salvation.

As I reflect on Paul's words to the Colossian church, I am reminded in Ecclesiastes that there is nothing new under the sun. Humanity plays the same song over and over as we search for life's meaning. There are philosophers who purport to give life meaning, but Christianity is the only religion that bases hope on love and a life exchanged for ours. It is the only religion that does not depend on our good behavior or our good works but solely on the fact that while we were yet sinners, God sent His Son to die for us. It is the only religion that takes us out of the equation and causes us to fully surrender to the love of God. And it is only God's love that can make us fully alive, causing our hearts to beat again.

Beloved friends, we live in an age where we are pulled and tossed around with empty philosophies. It is tempting to be swept away with the tide of unbelief and fear and even other religions that promise hope and don't deliver. Jesus did not say He was one of many ways to the Father. He said He is the *only way*: *"I am the way and the truth and the life. No one comes to the Father except through me."* (John 14:6) He is our only hope. Paul addressed this issue with the fledging church in Ephesus:

> *And He gave some as apostles, and some as prophets, and some as evangelists, and some as pastors and teachers, for the equipping of the saints for the work of service, to the building up of the body of Christ; until we all attain to the unity of the faith, and of the knowledge of the Son of God, to a mature man, to the measure of the stature which belongs to the fullness of Christ. As a result, we are no longer to be children, tossed here and there by*

waves and carried about by every wind of doctrine, by the trickery of men, by craftiness in deceitful scheming; but speaking the truth in love, we are to grow up in all aspects into Him who is the head, even Christ, from whom the whole body, being fitted and held together by what every joint supplies, according to the proper working of each individual part, causes the growth of the body for the building up of itself in love. (Eph. 4:11–16 NASB)

On Paul's second mission tour, he visited Ephesus after leaving Corinth, and planted the church there (Acts 18:19). *Ephesus* means "desirable," and in many ways it was a desirable place to live. It was located in west Asia Minor, near the sea.

On the third preaching journey, Paul spent between two and three years teaching in the city (Acts 19:8–10). He spent his time weeding out false doctrines and pagan practices. Ephesus derived its greatness from two sources, commercial trade and religion. During the Roman period it was a center for the mother goddess worship, known to the Greeks as Artemis and to the Romans as Diana. The superstitious Ephesians believed that Diana fell down from heaven. The temple of Diana was built about 400 BC, and worshippers engaged in immoral practices with the temple priestesses. Nevertheless, Paul's preaching in Ephesus was so successful that those who practiced magical arts brought their books (valued at fifty thousand pieces of silver) and burned them (Acts 19:18–20). This was the setting in which Paul warned against being tossed by waves and carried by every wind of doctrine. Today, we are faced with much of the same. It is easy to be tossed about by the waves of confusion. The simplicity of the gospel is lost in the pluralism of our society. There are so many doctrines that contradict the gospel. But just as the gospel exposed the false practices and doctrines in Ephesus for what they were, so the gospel still has the power to overcome the false ideas in our age. Yet God so loved the world that He came and broke through the confusion with His message of love.

The real issue that needs to be addressed is faith. If our faith is weak, we are easily tossed around in the sea of unbelief and confusion. What we need — what the church today needs — is renewed faith. We need mountain-moving faith to fend off our doubts and fears and to keep us from being tossed around by every wind of doctrine.

What thoughts and images come to mind when you think of mountains? I think of the Blue Ridge Mountains of North Carolina, where my husband and I spend a great deal of time hiking and enjoying the magnificent views. I think of the crisp air, the extravagant beauty of nature, and the breathtaking world God has created. When I think about mountains, I am also reminded of the mountaintop experiences in my life — like my wedding day, my children's births, and my children's weddings. All those mountaintop memories are engraved on my heart.

But mountains can bring negative images too. They can remind us, and represent for us, those things in our lives that can overwhelm us and seem insurmountable: illness, loss of loved ones, job struggles, mountains of debt, broken relationships.

Jesus understood all about mountains—both the peaks and the valleys. He knew the beauty of creation, and He saw the devastation of human sin and suffering. Using the mountain metaphor for those things in our lives that seem impossible or undefeatable, He taught His disciples, *"If you have faith as small as a mustard seed you can say to this mountain, 'Move from here to there' and it will move. Nothing will be impossible for you."* (Matt. 17:20)

That day, Jesus' disciples could not heal a young boy who was possessed by a demon. Jesus rebuked the demon and the boy was healed. He then told His followers that they needed to rely on God for the impossible — that mountains could be moved by faith. Moving mountains was a common metaphor in Jewish literature for doing what appeared to be impossible. In another teaching moment, Jesus demonstrated the possibilities of mountain-moving faith:

In the morning, as he was returning to the city, he became hungry. And seeing a fig tree by the wayside, he went to it and found nothing on it but only leaves. And he said to it, "May no fruit ever come from you again!" And the fig tree withered at once.

When the disciples saw it, they marveled saying, "How did the fig tree wither at once?" And Jesus answered them, "Truly, I say to you, if you have faith and do not doubt, you will not only do what has been done to the fig tree but even if you say to the mountain, 'Be taken up and thrown into the sea,' it will happen. And whatever you ask in prayer you will receive, if you have faith." (Matt. 21:18–22 ESV)

Jesus understood the mountains we face, and He demonstrated time and time again that prayers offered in faith could move them. There is something so intriguing to me about what Jesus said. He was giving us a key to prayer; He was saying that prayers must have power behind them, and that that power is faith. So this begs the question, how can we increase our faith? Romans 10:17 tells us that "faith comes from hearing, and hearing by the word of Christ" (NASB). So, knowing scripture, knowing how God has acted in the past and knowing His character from scripture builds faith. Additionally, as we begin to step out in obedience and faith, we will have our own experiences of God's power and character as we see Him acting in situations. These experiences of our own and others will build our faith as we see Him act in the present as He has in the past, moving in power in our lives and in the lives of others.

Faith and Prayer

I was once told that we know where we are on our spiritual journey if we examine where we spend our time, our money, and our talents. I must say I cringe some days to think of this. We fill our lives with things other than

God. But if we are to grow in our faith in Christ, it requires an investment in *His* kingdom, not the kingdom of the world.

We have said that our faith grows from spending time reading and meditating on God's Word. Another way to grow in our mountain-moving faith is through prayer. When we commune with God and we see answered prayer, our faith grows. Jesus grew in His relationship with His Father through prayer. He was never confused about what He came here to do because He went to spend time with His Father.

Scripture is full of passages that demonstrate the value Jesus placed on prayer. Throughout the Gospels we see Him getting alone with His Father to pray. Do you ever wonder what Jesus said? I find myself imagining His side of the conversation a lot:

"Dad, we had a good day today. Thank You for your faithfulness. Thank You showing me who You are and what You want every step of the way. I'm nothing without You. Thank You, too, for reminding me that nothing is impossible for You.

"The demoniac was delivered; the man by the pool of Siloam was healed. Another bad day with the Pharisees, though. I just don't fit into their religious box, do I, Dad? They got mad at me today because I healed on the Sabbath. But You told me that You are Lord of the Sabbath, right? I just tell them what You tell me.

"I am dog-tired today. Dad, give me strength to carry on. Thank You."

I imagine Jesus' conversations with His Dad were filled with thanksgiving, mixed with sorrow and compassion. He saw and talked to so many helpless people; He knew they were like sheep without a shepherd. (See Matt. 9:36). When He prayed in the Garden of Gethsemane on the night He was arrested, His soul was overwhelmed with dread and sorrow. (See Matt. 26:38; Mark 14:34). He shared with His Father all of what was on

His heart. He held nothing back. And He calls us to do the same. God is not a far-away deity we cannot approach. He is Love and Hope and Promise. He came to us and sacrificed Himself *for* us.

The Importance of Community

Another building block to our mountain-moving-faith is fellowship with other believers. It is easy to get confused and tossed around in a sea of doubt, but when you have the companionship of other devoted followers of Christ, you are better able to navigate the murky waters. In his book *Facets of Faith*, Everett Fullham emphasizes the importance of community.

> "This kind of communion shakes hell to its core because it drives the sword into the heart of despair (which is hell at its worst) and despair has no dominion over a communion of believers. I have seen men and women struggling as best they could to cope with the complexities of life by themselves, but galvanized into new people by the Holy Spirit at work in a local fellowship that draws strength from its members and from the Lord. Jesus told His disciples that when two or more are gathered in His Name, He is in their midst (Matthew 18:20). A community of believers working together is a force against the powers of darkness. It is imperative that we stay in fellowship working together for the expansion of the Kingdom of God. This was designed by God."[25]

The first-century church was dedicated to the Word, to communing with other Christians, and to prayer. The effect was like striking a match that ignited miracles. Acts 2:42 tells us, "They devoted themselves to the apostle's teachings and to fellowship, to the breaking of bread and to prayer. Everyone was filled with awe, and many wonders and miraculous signs were done by the apostles."

They lived expectantly, didn't they? Note that the verse says they devoted themselves to those practices, which is to say they *invested* themselves in them. They talked the talk; they walked the walk; they lived the life. Specifically, they were *devoted to prayer*. It wasn't something they fit into their schedule when it was convenient; it was the way they lived their lives.

The early church expected that God would show up. They were devoted to the teachings of scripture, prayer, and community. These practices kept them focused, built their faith, prevented them from being sidetracked with the philosophies of the day, and gave them support and encouragement. We must be built up in our faith by being rooted in the Word, devoted to prayer, and living in Christian community. As we are built up in our faith, our spiritual hearts will beat strong in sync with God's heart.

CHAPTER 14

Working from a Place of Rest

ACUTE STRESS CAN contribute to heart conditions. Again we see a similar pattern in our spiritual lives. Burning ourselves out and living for prolonged periods of time under stress damages our spiritual hearts. To all of you stressed-out, burned-out women, here is a word for you: *Just say no.* Say no to the things that you are not called to do -- the things that may be good but are not the best, the things that have been on life support. Just say no. It's really simpler than it seems. We are called to live and work from a place of rest — resting in Christ. God designed our spiritual hearts to be at rest in Him.

I mentioned before that the women I see in ministry are worn-out. We are trying to be all things to all people, and yet we are never satisfied. There is always more work to do. Always more people to connect with and always more on our plates than we can juggle at one time. It's time we learned that one of the secrets of kingdom living is to shed our old, overwhelmed selves and clothe ourselves in internal peace and rest. The Bible says some pretty profound things that address our need to slow down and rest.

In Exodus 18, Moses receives wise counsel from his father-in-law, Jethro. Moses acted as judge over Israel and would hear the people's cases. However, Jethro recognized that if Moses continued to do this without some help, he would burn out. Jethro advised Moses to delegate authority to some trustworthy men to help him hear the cases and provide justice. God had called Moses to do a particular task: lead the people out of Egypt and into the promised land. The other responsibilities needed to be delegated. Peace and rest were found when Moses was obedient to his call but did not exceed his call.

In the sixth chapter of Acts, the apostles in the early church also delegated tasks: they appointed deacons to help bear the burden of the ministry of the church. We must remember that God gives us a community of believers to work together, functioning as a whole. When the feeling of being overloaded bears down on us, we need to consider several things:

- Are we overstepping our God-given boundaries?
- Are we trusting God alone, or are we trying to be self-reliant?
- Are we willing to let go of control?
- Have we surrounded ourselves with people who are committed to come alongside and work together?
- Have we set ourselves up to be the savior trying to make all things right?

There is only one way we can move from self-reliance to God-reliance to peace and rest, and that is to focus on Jesus. The author of Hebrews wrote, "Let us run with perseverance the race marked out for us, fixing our eyes on Jesus, the pioneer and perfecter of faith" (Heb. 12:1–2).

We must stay connected to Jesus the Vine to avoid burnout. Only in Him can we move from *doing* to *being*. Our Western culture awards hard work, and there is nothing wrong with hard work. America was founded on individuals who had an outstanding work ethic. However, we have bought the lie that we must work overtime and rest only during our designated vacations, which may only be once or twice a year. As we grow in our relationship with Christ and our focus is on Him alone, we separate ourselves from the culture of stressed-out and begin working from a place of internal rest.

Jesus had a great conversation with a very busy woman named Martha, whom we mentioned earlier in the book. As you recall, Martha and her sister, Mary, had welcomed Jesus into their home, and Martha was busy with meal preparations. The problem is that Martha got lost in the preparations, while Mary got lost in Jesus. Martha was furious: "Lord, do you not care that my sister has left me to serve alone?" she complained. "Tell her then to help me."

But Jesus answered her, *"Martha, Martha, you are anxious and troubled about many things, but one thing is necessary. Mary has chosen the good portion, which will not be taken away from her."* (Luke 10:40–42)

We all know that life in the fast lane is not often fulfilling. We go so hard that we can hardly catch our breath, let alone spend time on ourselves or in nurturing our relationships with family and friends. We all dream about a time when we are not so busy. But then when we have a quiet moment, we don't know what to do with ourselves. We have been programmed to stay on the hamster wheel and have believed the lie that one day it will all be worth it.

Martha was doing what any of us would have done. She was preparing the best meal for her guest of honor. After all, this was the Messiah, the Miracle Worker, the one who had brought her brother, Lazarus, back from the dead. There was nothing she could do that would be enough to adequately express her love and thanksgiving to her friend. So she cooked, and she busied herself with the details of the dinner party.

Now, here is the thing: Martha was right: she had things to do, and she needed to do them. But when she complained to Jesus about Mary not helping, He did not rush to her defense. Instead He said, "Martha, Martha, you are worried and upset about many things, but only one thing is needed. Mary has chosen what is better."

Martha had work to do, but Jesus wanted her to prioritize her work; first Jesus, then work. The work will flow much easier from a place of rest. Perhaps Jesus could have said this to Martha: "If you want to be a better Martha, you must first be a better Mary and learn to work from a place of rest. Sounds counterintuitive, but I would put my bet on Jesus knowing the best and most efficient way of doing things.

Why is it that when people ask me how I'm doing, my most common response is "I'm busy?" Maybe you don't say that, but I do — all the time, it seems — and I hear a lot of other people saying the same thing. I have one friend who has a different answer to that question. He says, "I'm blessed." I like that reply better, yet more often than I care to admit, the I'm-busy one jumps out of my mouth before I've given it any thought.

How do we choose the "good portion"? By doing what Mary did. Mary chose the one needed thing, to sit at the feet of Jesus. First she sat at his feet; then she worked from a place of rest. Beloved women, to be a better Martha, we must each first be a better Mary. When we are connected to Jesus the Vine and are first refreshed by His Presence, we feel more alive and are less likely to experience burnout. In fact, from a position of making space for God, receiving our fill from Him, we are less likely to push the limits of what we can do or are called to do and more likely to hear and only do the things God calls us to do.

Today my husband gave me a cycling lesson. He bought me a new bike, and he was trying to teach me how to ride with toe clips. I must say I was less than enthused about being clipped into the pedals, knowing that if I fell it would be awful. I did fall. I couldn't get my feet out of the toe clips—not that it was difficult to do. I just froze. I was thinking as I fell, *I am falling, and there is nothing I can do about it.* There *was* something I could do about it, but all I kept thinking about was falling, not about unclipping my shoes. For those of you readers who are hard-core cyclists, hats off to you. But I am finished. Never to see those toe clips again.

As I reflected on this chapter, I realized that having my toes in toe clips can be compared to spinning and spinning, tied into the cycle of busyness, knowing all I have to do is unclip my shoes but being too focused on the spinning. With little effort I could have released my toes. And with little effort we can stop the madness and prevent a fall. Burnout is not fun. For those of you have experienced it or who are experiencing this right now, you know what I mean. Your job can become monotonous, losing its freshness, whether you are working outside the home or a stay-at-home mom or single or whatever. Spinning out of control is not fun. It's like falling off a bicycle. Not worth the price.

Jesus' words remind us that it is in trusting Him that we can stop the madness. We need not be overwhelmed:

> And he said to his disciples, "Therefore I tell you, do not be anxious about your life, what you will eat, nor about your body, what you will put on. For life is more than food, and the body more than clothing. Consider the ravens: they neither sow nor reap, they have neither storehouse nor barn, and yet God feeds them. Of how much more value are you than the birds! And which of you by being anxious can add a single hour to his span of life? If then you are not able to do as small a thing as that, why are you anxious about the rest? Consider the lilies, how they grow: they neither toil nor spin, yet I tell you, even Solomon in all his glory was not arrayed like one of these. But if God so clothes the grass, which is alive in the field today, and tomorrow is thrown into the oven, how much more will he clothe you, O you of little faith! And do not seek what you are to eat and what you are to drink, nor be worried. For all the nations of the world seek after these things, and your Father knows that you need them. Instead, seek his kingdom, and these things will be added to you.
>
> Fear not, little flock, for it is your Father's good pleasure to give you the kingdom." (Luke 12:22–32 ESV)

Jesus tells us not to fear, and He sees spinning and toil as the by-products of our fear; we are not trusting Him. Again, a good work ethic is commendable. It is when work becomes our god that we begin to spin out of control. When our work causes us internally to implode, we know we are in trouble. Jesus calls us to seek His kingdom first, and all the other things will be added (Matt. 6:33). He calls us to be filled with His presence so that we can work from a place of rest. When we are filled, we work from a place of simply pouring out what He has given us.

I am a reformed workaholic. When I recognized that *doing* had replaced my *being* with God, I knew I was in trouble. My stress level rose, and my impatience was a sure sign that something was wrong. I had replaced the secret place with the place of high performance. I had sacrificed my time with God on the altar of people pleasing. And I imagine that some of you have done the same thing. I was empty, and tired, and burned-out. Nothing seemed enough. But God never forsakes us. He drew me back with cords of love and made me thirst for His presence. Only He can fill the God-shaped hole in our hearts. And only He can cause our hearts to beat again.

I want to address all of you married women who are worn-out. Maybe your job has depleted you, and there is little time or energy left over for your husband. Maybe you have children and a job, and you are running on half empty. Perhaps you have poured yourself into other relationships, and your husband gets what is left over. I have been married for more than forty years, and I will tell you the secret of a happy marriage: make space for God, and from that place, make space for your spouse. That's right: first God, then your husband, then family, your job and so forth. Our families need us to be refreshed and filled and not stressed-out. If you have made big space for God in your life, you can count on peace residing in your home; and you can work from a place of internal rest. Sure, you can be Martha. I like to be Martha. But in order to be a better Martha, you need to be a better Mary.

We have come to the end of our journey together. Let's review. God is calling us to wake up (be resuscitated), rise up (be repositioned), and grow up (be renewed) to become the city on a hill in a world that needs Christ. We have become weary in the journey, forgetting that the only way for our hearts to beat with purpose is to have them beating with *passion* for Christ. To do this, we must let go of the old — our old self-life — and embrace our new life in Christ, clothed with His love, so we can release His hope to others in need. We have taken on the stress of the world, but it's time that we reposition our lives, recognizing that we are glory-carriers, vessels of God's presence. We are temples of His Holy Spirit, meant to shine with *His glory* in a world that's dark.

The church is not irrelevant or outdated. Clothed with compassion and filled with Christ, it can be a world changer. As we stay connected to Jesus, the Vine, we will find that our weary, stressed-out lives are refreshed, and we can, in turn, refresh others. As we make space for God, we will do our work, including kingdom work, from a place of resting in Him, no longer tossed around in a sea of confusion. Our lives take on meaning and hope.

We must be determined to press on in our spiritual journey — keep climbing so that we get a God-perspective. We must take time *to be with Jesus.*

When Mary made time and space to sit at her Master's feet, she worshiped and adored Him. She knew that in Him all her needs were met. But what she may not have known is that He wanted to be her *friend.*

Before Jesus ascended to heaven, He told His disciples that He no longer called them servants; He called them *friends* (John 15:15). How strange that must have sounded to them. The King of kings, their Master, was calling them friends.

He calls you friend too. Yes, you. He wants to go back to the garden of Eden — the place where it all began — and walk with you in the cool of the evening and just be your friend. Things got messed up in the garden. A spirit of rebellion snuck in, and for a while (seemed like an eternity) mankind and God were separated. But the God of the universe — who calls you *friend* — found a way to reunite you and Him. He could not bear the thought of not having you as His friend. Yes, you. And when we are united to Him as friends, our hearts will beat again, and we will know what it is like to be fully alive. When we live as He designed us to live, from a place of rest in Him, abiding in Him, doing only those things that He put on our plate, giving Him our burdens and taking on His easy yoke, our hearts will be at peace and beat with the steady rhythm of grace.

Notes

Introduction

1. Randy Phillips with Phillips, Craig and Dean, "Tell Your Heart to Beat Again," released on June 23, 2014 in *Hope in Front of Me*, BGM Records.

Chapter 3

2. Brenda Goodman, MA, "For Multiple Heart Blockages, Bypass Surgery of Stents?" *Web MD*, (March 16, 2011): http://www.webmd.com/heart-disease/news/20110316/for-multiple-heart-blockages-bypass-surgery-or-stents?

3. *Merriam-Webster Medical Dictionary*, s.v. "revitalize," http://www.merriam-webster.com/dictionary/revitalize, accessed July 15, 2015.

4. *Wikipedia*, "Arteriosclerosis," https://en.wikipedia.org/wiki/Arteriosclerosis, accessed February 27, 2016.

Chapter 4

5. *Medicine Net*, "What to Expect During a Heart Transplant," http://www.medicinenet.com/stress/page3.htm#what_are_the_signs_and_symptoms_of_poorly_managed_stress, accessed September 2, 2015.

6. Joseph S. Carroll, *How to Worship Jesus Christ*, Moody ed. (Chicago: Moody, 1991), 19–20.

7. Dallas Willard, *Renovation of the Heart* (Navpress Publishing, 2012), 209.

8. C.S. Lewis, *Reflections on the Psalms* (Harvest Book, 1964), 90-91.
9. A. W. Tozer, *Today in the Word*, December 2003, p. 8.
10. Matt Redman, "The Heart of Worship," released in 1998 on *Intimacy*, Survivor Records (UK), and in 1999 on *Heart of Worship*, Star Song (US), studio album.

Chapter 5

11. Bruce Wilkinson, *The Dream Giver* (Colorado Springs: Multnomah, 2003), 29–30.

Chapter 6

12. Bishop Irenaeus, Against Heresies (185 AD).
13. Philip Keller, *A Shepherd Looks at Psalm 23* (Grand Rapids: Zondervan, 1970; 2007), 51–52.

Chapter 7

14. Mark Harris, "Find Your Wings," from the album *The Line Between the Two*, producer Peter Kipley, Fair Trade/Provident, 2005.
15. Andy Andrews, *The Travelers Gift: Seven Decisions That Determine Personal Success* (Nashville: Thomas Nelson, 2002), 154–55.

Chapter 9

16. John Eldredge, *Waking the Dead: The Glory of a Heart Fully Alive* (Nashville: Thomas Nelson, 2003), 2.

17. Ibid., 12–13.
18. Tom White, *The Believer's Guide to Spiritual Warfare* (Ventura, CA: Regal, 2011), 180.

Chapter 10

19. Oswald Chambers, *My Utmost for His Highest (Grand Rapids, Michigan: Discovery House Publishers),14.*

Chapter 11

20. Medicine Plus Medical Encyclopedia, http://www.nhlbi.nih.gov/health/health-topics/topics/ht/during, accessed February 27, 2016.

Chapter 12

21. Joyce Landorf Heatherley, *Balcony People*, rev. ed. (Georgetown, TX: Balcony, 2004), 9.
22. Ibid., 9.

Chapter 13

23. C. S. Lewis, *The Screwtape Letters*, repr. ed. (New York: HarperCollins, 2001), 82.
24. Arthur S. Peake, A *Commentary on the Bible (London: T.C. & E.C. Jack, 1920).*
25. Fullham, Everett, *Facets of Faith* (Chosen Books, 1982), 106.

About the Author

FOUNDER OF INTERNATIONAL nonprofit Drawing Near to God based in Mt. Pleasant, S.C., Joanne Ellison teaches women to make space for God so that God's presence keeps them from being overwhelmed with life.

Driven by a vision to motivate women to pursue a deeper relationship with God, Ellison founded Drawing Near to God in 2000 and has since reached tens of thousands of women through Christian radio, television, her weekly Bible study, speaking, books, CDs and DVDs. She is the author of over 20 Bible study guides, the popular 365-day Bible devotional, Drawing Near To God, Sitting at His Feet and Tell Your Heart to Beat Again.

Ellison is an engaging speaker, writer and Bible teacher. Her speaking style includes both vulnerability and humor and is rooted in her passion for the Bible.

She is a mother of three, grandmother of 11 and has been married for 44 years to Dr. Blount Ellison. Making her home in the Charleston area for most of her life, Ellison is a graduate of the College of Charleston and an active member of Saint Andrew's Church, Mount Pleasant, SC.